CONGREGATION
FOR INSTITUTES OF CONSECRATED LIFE
AND SOCIETIES OF APOSTOLIC LIFE

The Art of Seeking the Face of God

Guidelines for the Formation of Women Contemplatives

"Your face, Lord, do I seek" (*Ps* 27:8)

On the cover:
San Damiano Crucifix
© Protomonastery of St. Clare (Assisi)

International Copyright handled by
Libreria Editrice Vaticana
00120 Città del Vaticano
Tel. +39 06.698.45780 - Fax +39 06.698.84716
E-mail: commerciale.lev@spc.va

ISBN: 978-88-266-0477-0
www.libreriaeditricevaticana.va

Seeking the face of God
has always been a part of our human history.
From the beginning, men and women have been
called to a dialogue of love with the Creator.

Indeed, mankind is distinguished
by an irrepressible religious dimension
that leads human hearts to feel the need
to seek God, the Absolute.

In seeking God,
we quickly realize that no one is self-sufficient.
Rather, we are called,
in the light of faith,
to move beyond self-centeredness,
drawn by God's Holy Face and
by the "sacred ground of the other",
to an ever more profound experience of communion.

(FRANCIS, *Vultum Dei quaerere,* I, 1)

The need for formation

1. Contemplative life rooted in silence, initial form of communities of consecrated life in the Church, unfolds seeking the Face of God, while it witnesses and contemplates it in the world's heart. Even in the simplicity of their lives, cloistered communities, set like cities on a hilltop or lights on a lampstand (cf. *Matt.* 5:14-15), visibly represent the goal towards which the entire community of the Church is aimed at. The Church "advances down the paths of time with her eye fixed on the future restoration of all things in Christ."[1]

2. In the Apostolic Constitution *Vultum Dei quaerere,* Pope Francis presents this ultimate mystery to the entire Church, while confirming the experience of contemplative women, who centered on the Lord as their

[1] John Paul II, Post-Synodal Apostolic Exhortation *Vita consecrata,* (March 25, 1996), 59.

first and only love (cf. *Hos.* 2:21-25), have brought forth abundant fruits of holiness and great apostolic efficacy.[2] In this overview, full of care, Francis favors formation as a necessary process to support and enliven the vocational path today.[3]

3. The need for formation is part of a broad horizon that goes beyond the walls of monasteries, that embraces the world, that calls for living with intelligence, communion in heart and practice, and urges the assessment of limits and apparent separations. The Holy Father, aware that "no one contributes to the future in isolation, by his or her efforts alone"[4], calls to avoid the "disease of self-referentiality"[5] and to cherish the value of communion among different monasteries as a path towards the future, and thereby updating and implementing the

[2] Cf. FRANCIS, Ap. Const. *Vultum Dei quaerere*, (June 29, 2016), 5.

[3] Cf. *Ivi*, Conclusion and regulations, art. 3-8.

[4] FRANCIS, *Apostolic Letter* to all Consacrated people on the occasion of the Year of Consecrated Life, (November 21, 2014), II.

[5] *Ivi*.

permanent and values of autonomy codified.[6] The constant search for the face of God, on a personal and community level, makes communion fruitful, thus becoming the vital and generative environment for formation.

4. The following *Guidelines* provide simple directions for the formation of nuns according to the specific need, in order to support the journey of contemplative women,[7] pilgrim women seeking the true God, "the praying heart in the Church and for the Church",[8] outpost of humanity and parable of the Kingdom of Heaven. Within this context, the present *Ratio* offers a tool to foster integral human development, through human and spiritual formation, in order to achieve and strengthen a full maturity in Christ. It involves a hand

[6] Cf. *Ivi*; CIC, cann. 614-615; 628§2-1; 630§3; 638§4; 684§3; 688§2; 699§2; 708; 1428§1-2.

[7] In this document the words nuns and contemplative women are used interchangeably, so as to respect different sensitivities.

[8] Congregation for Institutes of consecrated life and Societies of apostolic life, *Cor orans.* Implementing instruction on women's contemplative life, (April 1, 2018), Introduction.

crafted work,[9] a process, which requires "a large space of time".[10]

[9] Cf. FRANCIS, *The Strength of a Vocation. Consecrated Life Today*. Conversation with FERNANDO PRADO, 2, CCF, 2018, 75.

[10] JOHN PAUL II, Post-synodal Ap. Ex. *Vita consecrata,* (March 25, 1996), 65.

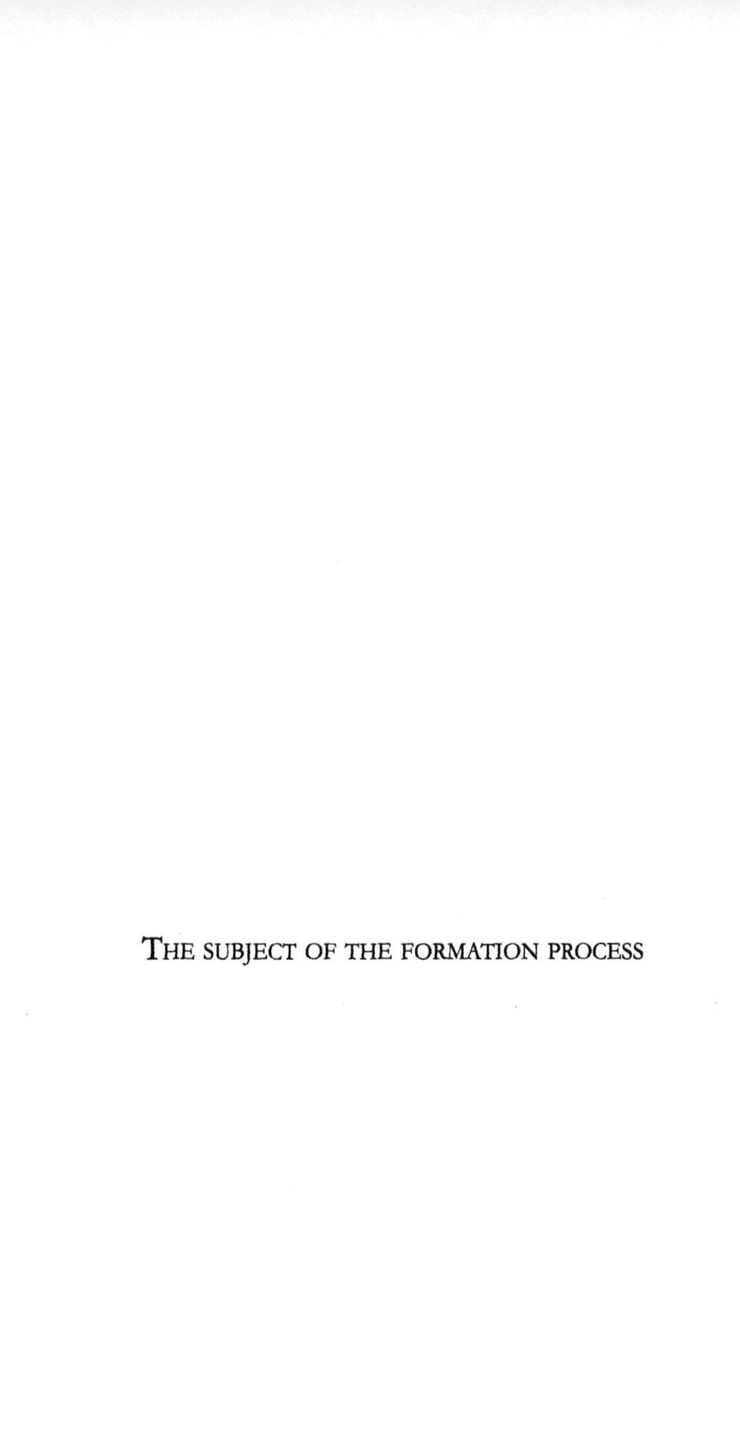

THE SUBJECT OF THE FORMATION PROCESS

In becoming vital

5. The monastery is "a school of the Lord's service." The term school offers the right and inspirational vision of these *Guidelines*, placing the formation process in a permanent and stable place in order to live rooted in silence with consciousness and fidelity, without hidden escapes.[1]

This never-ending formation process is in continuous development,[2] leading *to mature manhood, to the extent of the mature stature of Christ* (*Eph.* 4:13). It cannot be limited to conveying notions and learning attitudes and behaviors, but opens a full horizon, accompanying human, Christian, and monastic maturity without juxtaposition or parallel instances.

[1] Cf. CONGREGATION FOR INSTITUTES OF CONSECRATED LIFE AN SOCIETIES OF APOSTOLIC LIFE, *Cor orans*. Implementation instructions of the apostolic constitution on Women's Contemplative life, (April 1, 2018), 18.

[2] Cf. JOHN PAUL II, Post-Synodal Ap. Ex. *Vita consecrata,* (March 25, 1996), 65.

6. The formation process, a conscious and vital activity for each person, offers all contemplative women the possibility to grow humanly and spiritually. Consciousness, fostered by daily exercise, accompanies growth in the spirit so that the person can proceed towards full awareness of her being. Despite the continuous flow of thoughts, emotions and feelings, the person's core identity remains unaltered because she lives according to the meaning of her vocation: seeking the face of God, living the Gospel, taking care of the relationship with the Lord, with herself, the sisters and the men and women of our time.

Self-awareness plays an irreplaceable part in the life of the person who becomes a conscious and responsible subject of her existence. Only by being self-aware can one know, believe, love, and humanly relate to reality and to the transcendent.

The development of conscience

7. Human consciousness is neither steady nor straightforward because it is structured and differs, and develops over time and in different contexts. The development of the person, of being attentive, intelligent, rational, responsible and living in different spheres is a continuous process of construction and modification of conscious life.

8. Every contemplative woman is the primary target of this formation process, which leads her to self-awareness and to freely, creatively and faithfully collaborate in the formational aspects of her stage in life. As she progresses in monastic life, she is called to trust her heart in addressing desires and agitations resolutely. It is a beautiful and demanding commitment, that from the very beginning of the monastic journey, calls for lifelong self-awareness and honesty.

9. Saint Benedict begins the *Rule* suggesting "to establish nothing harsh, nor burdensome" and continues "but, if suggested by a reasonable balance, may be introduced in order to amend faults and to safeguard charity";[3] thus, one must not flee, but persevere. It is an integral and integrated formation path, as a continual process of conversion, enlightenment, and transfiguration, where the action of the Holy

[3] Benedict, *The Rule,* Prologue, 45-47.

Spirit turns us into *real children of God* (*1Jn.* 3:1) and liberates us from *the yoke of slavery* (*Gal* 5:1).

The goal is not that of mortification, but to transform the whole being into the image of God through contemplation[4] and thus opening up to the art of real self-giving, being available to die in order to grow in the freedom of giving oneself, for a bigger love that enlarges the heart (cf. *Ps.* 119:32)[5] and opens it to the action of the Holy Spirit.[6]

10. The serene and courageous acceptance of the transformations that accompany and sometimes unexpectedly mark life makes the contemplative sister ever more aware of the path she goes through in the mystery of the given vocation: "Nor, while ascending, do we cease to desire more, knowing what we know. Rather, as we rise by a greater desire to one still

[4] Cf. Clare of Assisi, *III Letter to St. Agnes of Prague*, 13.

[5] In this context Pope Francis warns against "a conception a bit Pelagian of consecrated life" that leads it to lose "some of its freshness", cf. Francis, *The Strength of a Vocation. Consecrated life today.* Conversation with Fernando Prado, 2, CCF, 2018, 49.

[6] Cf. John Paul II, Post-Synodal Ap. Ex. *Vita consecrata,* (March 25, 1996), 65.

higher, we continue our way into the infinite by increasingly higher ascents",[7] assuming Christ as: "All: the Good, all Good, Supreme Good".[8]

11. Contemplative religious sisters accept the challenge of the formation of conscience which – like any human journey – by its nature is a long path towards perfection, according to the identity and peculiarities which grace makes fruitful in each person. Being formed means welcoming in "*jars of clay*" (*2Cor* 4:7) the Trinitarian mystery that inhabits us, according to the Apostle's exhortation: *"In your relationships with one another, have the same mindset as Christ Jesus"* (*Phil.* 2:5).

The identity of a disciple

12. The primary objective of the formation of contemplative sisters emerges from the process of human formation: to establish the identity of disciples of Christ in the evangelical and specific charismatic vocation, harmonizing all human aspects in the wholeness of the spirit. The path to conform to Christ till *achiev-*

[7] Gregory of Nyssa, *Homilies on the Song of Songs,* PG 44, 941 C.

[8] Francis of Assisi, *Prasie to God Almighty,* 3.

ing the attitude of Christ towards the Father[9], is an open process which does not end with initial formation but continues at every stage of life. It calls for personal planning in line with the evolutionary phase of each member who continually bears witness to the adventure of Christian humanity in the monastic form.

13. On this journey, the spiritual woman develops by living the advice of the Gospel, in daily decisions, like harmony and lifestyle. The goal can be achieved through an "hand crafted work"[10] of self-formation; she "proceeds along the path already trodden by Virgin Mary, who advanced in her pilgrimage of faith, and loyally persevered in her union with her Son unto the Cross".[11] It is a life project where the concrete aspect of everyday life has a specific and irreplaceable role, in the logic of the incarnation. By doing so, the woman gradually acquires the

[9] JOHN PAUL II, Post-Synodal Ap. Ex. *Vita consecrata,* (March 25, 1996), 65.

[10] A. SPADARO, *"Svegliate il mondo!". Colloquio di Papa Francesco con i Superiori Generali,* in: *La Civiltà Cattolica,* 165 (2014/I), 10 ("Wake up the World! Conversation with Pope Francis with General Superiors").

[11] JOHN PAUL II, Enc. Lett. *Redemptoris Mater,* (March 25, 1987), 2.

peculiar identity of monastic life in the mystery of the holiness of the Church, becoming a "sign of the exclusive union of the Church as Bride with her Lord, whom she loves above all things".[12]

14. Anthony the *Abbot* reminds us of the need to constantly enter into the awareness of the reasons of our choice: today, I start anew. It is a fruitful and constant process that occurs every day as we enter barefooted the *holy land* (*Ex.* 3:5) of reality, avoiding a hardening heart: *Today, if only you would hear his voice! Do not harden your hearts* (*Ps.* 95:7-8). Without a conscious and peaceful contact with reality, without *docility* and a meek and humble heart, a stable and lasting formation process cannot be started.

15. Therefore, every true formation is demanding and strict because it is an experience of the total gift of love, starting from the word of Jesus: *the truth will set you free* (*Jn.* 8:32). It involves starting from the truth about oneself and fraternal life lived concretely. This freedom which generates love allows adoration of the

[12] John Paul II, Post-Synodal Ap. Ex. *Vita consecrata*, (March 25, 1996), 59.

Lord, Christ, in your hearts and to give an account for the hope that is in us (cf. *1Pt* 3:15) and, at the same time, to offer a generative contribution to fraternal life in community.

16. This life-giving path is bound to be gradual and lasting throughout the entire life, in the personal awareness and constant openness to grace, starting from vocational accompaniment to the preparation of meeting the God of life in the ultimate moment of death.

Formation to contemplative life

Formation dimensions

17. *"Come, let us go up to the mountain of the Lord, to the house where the God of Jacob dwells. He will teach us his ways* (*Is* 2:3). Yes, come with me, my thoughts, will and desires, let us go up to that mountain: that is where the Lord looks down on us and where we gaze on the Lord".[1] If the call to contemplation, to climb the mountain of the Lord, is the vocation of the Church and in her all other activity is directed and subordinated,[2] this takes on a permanent meaning and emphasis for monastic communities, praying communities wholly dedicated to contemplation, according to the specific charism of each religious family.

[1] WILLIAM OF SAINT THIERRY, *On Contemplating God*, Prologue, 1.

[2] Cf. ECUM. COUNCIL VATICAN II, Constitution on the Sacred Liturgy *Sacrosanctum Concilium*, 2; Cf. FRANCIS OF ASSISI, *Earlier Rule*, XXII-XXIII.

18. Contemplative monastic life, *sequela pressius Christi*,[3] is radically focused on "the never ending search for God".[4] This mystery of life requires a continuous process of integration and unification and calls for certain formation elements of its own.[5] It includes making sure that everything about a person is integrated in a harmonious and balanced way, in line with the vision of a sound and correct anthropological theology,[6] living without dichotomy the intellectual and emotional formation, individual and communitarian, personal and social, affective and sexual.

19. Formation in the contemplative life requires the person to be accompanied so that thinking, loving, and acting according to the Spirit become the norm that manifests itself

[3] Cf. Francis, Ap. Con. *Vultum Dei quaerere*, (June 29, 2016), 1-3.

[4] Cf. *Ivi*, 3.

[5] Cf. Congregation for Institues of consecrated life and Societies of apostolic life, Directives on formation in Religious Institutes *Potissimum Institutioni*, Rome, (February 2, 1990), 72-80.

[6] Cf. *Ivi*, 76.77.79.80.81.

in a profoundly human evangelical style.[7] Accompaniment always begins from the specific reality of each sister.

20. During accompaniment, besides sisters in initial formation, specific attention must be paid to the sisters in the first years of solemn vows and the sisters in difficulty, turning, when considered convenient or necessary, to joint spiritual and psychological accompaniment.

21. Accompaniment calls for an environment of trust and familiarity so that the accompanier, like a "mother", learns how to "love and care" for the accompanied sister,[8] by always being a close companion on the journey, welcoming the sister in her reality and promoting her positive attitudes.

22. In this environment, the accompanied sister can open her heart to the *older* sister or brother that the Lord has put by her side to share the journey she is undertaking of following Christ, the joy of the same vocation and can

[7] Cf. Francis, *The Strength of a Vocation. Consecrated Life Today.* Conversation with Fernando Prado, 2, CCF, 2018, 74-76.

[8] Cf. Francis of Assisi, *Regula Bollata*, 6, 7.

manifest, at the same time, "with confidence her own needs to the other".[9]

23. The one who accompanies must be aware that her/his ministry is a service to foster growth in human and vocational maturity; being respectful and sensitive of the sister's mystery; she/he should be adequately spiritually and pedagogically prepared to carry out the task; having herself/himself been accompanied and transmitting, especially with the life, her/his joyful belonging to God in a specific charism.

24. In turn, the accompanied sister must bear in mind that accompaniment is a journey of *dispossession* and *restitution*, and as such it must acknowledge her weaknesses and fragilities. Self-discovery, as a human being in need of salvation, forgiveness and light, is the starting point for an authentic formation process.

Integral human development

25. In order to be such, formation needs to address the person in her truest human essence, leading her to the true knowledge of self,

[9] Cf. SAINT FRANCIS OF ASSISI, *Regula Bollata*, 6, 7.

her gifts, and limitations. By doing so, she will be helped to achieve the inner freedom needed to live her consecration consistently and honestly, with serenity and joy, generosity, and charity,[10] both within the community and in relationship with the external world. There is no formation growth without a life that shapes the vocation, that fulfills God's plan for the person.

26. The journey of self-knowledge is especially precious in the formation to ascetic commitment, an essential aspect of contemplative life, gift and "natural response to the first and only love".[11] It helps by enabling all the human elements of each sister to fully flourish, avoiding the risk of discouraging her with dynamics which are immature and self-centered or excessively sacred and outdated. The first step is undoubtedly anthropological, and calls each person to be welcomed as a historical human being, acknowledging her limits and wounds.

27. The contemplative sister, like all consecrated persons, needs someone to accom-

[10] Cf. JOHN PAUL II, Post-synodal Ap. Ex. *Vita consecrata,* (March 25, 1996), 71.

[11] Cf. FRANCIS, Ap. Const. *Vultum Dei quaerere,* (June 29, 2016), 35.

pany and support her along her self-reconciliation path, taking special care "of the human and emotional maturity".[12] In this context, it is fundamental for the sister in ongoing or initial formation to become aware of herself, of her body, femininity, affectivity, always directing them to the vocational choice.

28. Since the human aspect of the person is shaped through relationships, the formative action must specifically consider three levels of relationships:

– With herself:

* favoring a re-reading of her story and reconciliation with her past, which will make her a free person, to continue to discover in current events, the work of God in her;
* acquiring an ever more stable balance by taking into consideration the rhythms of daily life, learning to read in the small and great daily events the continuous presence of God "making everything new" (*Rev* 21:5);
* acquiring appropriate self-esteem and care of the inner self and body, harmonizing

[12] FRANCIS, *The Strength of a Vocation. Consecrated Life Today*. Conversation with FERNANDO PRADO, 2, CCF, 2018, 82.

and unifying her feminine resources to the vocational choice;

* completely overcoming any form of dependence, both to social media and the previous lifestyle, assimilating the lifestyle of the new community.

– With her sisters and with others:

* discovering the joy of fraternal life in community, living according to one's charism, and developing and consolidating a sense of belonging to it;
* experiencing gratuitousness and self-giving in relationships, welcoming the other sisters as gifts from God;
* cultivating fundamental human qualities for living relationships;
* acquiring a constructive critical sense from a faith-based logic;
* developing the abilities to communicate, harmonizing words and silence and adequately tackling conflicts;
* being sensitive to the forms of poverty and marginalization of today's world and, by contemplating Jesus' predilection for the poor, showing solidarity to them by offering prayers and those acts of charity which the Holy Spirit may suggest.

– With creation:

* acquiring a sober and respectful use of things, which allows her to overcome the consumerist throw-away mentality;
* learning to draw from nature the reasons for contemplation and praise, to have a healthy relationship with it as a source of psycho-physical balance, rediscovering the beauty and goodness of creation coming out of the hands of God and respecting it at all times;
* experiencing work as a grace that permits each sister to participate in the mystery of God's creation and to share the fatigue of the poor.

29. Self-knowledge, aimed at a sincere gift of self and one's own life,[13] in behavior and intentions,[14] develops in the logic of communion,[15] is realized in daily life, in the context

[13] Cf. JOHN PAUL II, Ap. Lett. *Mulieris dignitatem*, (August 15, 1988), 7.

[14] Cf. JOHN PAUL II, Post-Synodal Ap. Ex. *Vita consecrata*, (March 25, 1996), 65.

[15] Cf. CONGREGATION FOR INSTITUES OF CONSECRATED LIFE AND SOCIETIES OF APOSTOLIC LIFE: Instruction *Starting afresh from Christ: a renewed commitment to consecrated*

of a monastery in which the concreteness and evangelical quality of relationships are a source of fertility.[16] This humanity activates the awareness of one's own Baptism by which every believer is immersed in the Mystery of Christ, in a renewed dynamism of conversion, fruit of docility to the work of the Spirit.

30. The monastery, always described as a "workshop"[17] of practical apprenticeship for purity of heart and life, "a school of the divine service"[18] and school of charity, becomes a place of ongoing formation in conversion and asceticism.[19] Inner maturity goes through an inner struggle (cf. *Eph.* 6:10-20), the exercise of discernment (cf. *Phil.* 2:5-11; *1 Cor.* 2:15; 12:10),

life in the third millennium, (May 19, 2002), 28; John Paul II, Ap. Lett. *Novo Millennio Ineunte*, (January 6, 2001), 43.

[16] Cf. John Paul II, *Speech* to the participants of the Plenary Assembly of the Congregation for institues of consecrated life and Societies of apostolic life, (November 20, 1992) (IT).

[17] Benedict, *Rule,* 4,78.

[18] *Ivi*, Prologue, 45

[19] Cf. Congregation for Institues of consecrated life and Societies of apostolic life, Directives on formation in Religious Institutes *Potissimum Institutioni*, Rome, (February 2, 1990), 36-38.

the experience of the Cross and the acquisition of the wisdom of the Paschal Mystery.[20]

31. Monastic consecration features constant search and continuous growth to avoid spiritual sclerosis. Throughout the process, specific care should be given to a balanced growth of both the spiritual and human dimension, that "involves paying attention to the specific anthropology of the various cultures and the sensitivity of new generations, with particular focus on new contexts of life".[21] In the formative dynamics, it can be appropriate, in cases of real need, to make use of the help of experts in human sciences. These experiences cannot replace specific discernment on monastic life with the personal accompaniment of formators and cordial dialogue with those serving in authority.

[20] Cf. *Ivi*, 36-38; Cf. JOHN PAUL II, Post-Synodal Ap. Ex. *Vita consecrata,* (March 25, 1996), 38

[21] CONGREGATION FOR INSTITUES OF CONSECRATED LIFE AND SOCIETIES OF APOSTOLIC LIFE, *New Wine in New Wineskins.* The Consecrated life and its ongoing challenges since Vatican II. Guidelines, (January 6, 2017), 14.

32. Monastic formation is an essential theological activity, rooted in the Holy Spirit, in its source and its aims. It proposes a journey to reach communion with the one and Triune God, while calling to the primary task of the praise of God lived in fullness.[22]

33. The *Opus Dei* and the Eucharist are *fons et culmen* of the Church's life and contemplative life.[23] The liturgy "is both human and divine, visible and yet invisibly equipped, eager to act and yet intent on contemplation, present in this world and yet not at home in it; and she is all these things in such wise that in her the human is directed and subordinated to the divine, the visible likewise to the invisible, action to contemplation, and this present world to that city yet to come, which we seek".[24] Daily litur-

[22] Cf. Congregation for Institues of consecrated life and Societies of apostolic life, Directives on formation in Religious Institutes *Potissimum Institutioni*, Rome, (February 2, 1990), 77.

[23] Cf. Francis, Ap. Const. *Vultum Dei quaerere*, (June 29, 2016), I, 22-23.

[24] Cf. Ecumenical Council Vatican II, Constitution on the Sacred Liturgy *Sacrosanctum Concilium*, 2.

gy must be prepared and celebrated with care, avoiding the risk of being self-absorbed and monotonous.[25]

34. "Contemplative men and women, with their life of prayer, listening and meditating the Word of God, remind us that man does not live on bread alone, but on every word that comes from the mouth of God (cf. *Matt.* 4:4)".[26] The prayerful reading of the Word constantly renews the encounter with God.[27] Contemplative sisters prepare themselves for *lectio divina* by adequate biblical studies. Through daily exercise[28] they improve their ability to understand the Scriptures (cf. *Lk.* 24:27).

The Scripture becomes the source of knowledge for the mystery of Christ and man. Saint Jerome's phrase, cited also in Vatican Council II,

[25] Cf. FRANCIS, Ap. Const. *Vultum Dei quaerere*, (June 29, 2016), I, 16.

[26] Cf. BENEDICT XVI, Post-Synodal Apostolic Exhortation *Verbum Domini*, (September 30, 2010), 83.

[27] Cf. FRANCIS, Ap. Const. *Vultum Dei quaerere*, (June 29, 2016) I, 19-21.

[28] Cf. *Ivi*, 19-20; CONGREGATION FOR INSTITUES OF CONSECRATED LIFE AND SOCIETIES OF APOSTOLIC LIFE, Directives on formation in Religious Institutes *Potissimum Institutioni*, Rome, (February 2, 1990), 76.

is still true: "For ignorance of the Scriptures is ignorance of Christ".[29]

35. *Lectio divina* is not a devotional practice like other forms of personal prayer but a condition *sine qua non* of contemplative life: "Diligently apply yourself to reading the sacred Scriptures. Apply yourself, I say. And applying yourself thus to study the things of God, with faithful prejudgments such as are well pleasing to God, knock at its locked door, and it will be opened to you by the porter, of whom Jesus says, 'To him, the porter opens'. And applying yourself thus to divine reading, seek aright and with unwavering trust in God the meaning of holy Scriptures, which so many have missed. Be not satisfied with knocking and seeking; for prayer is of all things indispensable to the knowledge of the things of God. For this the Savior exhorted, and said not only, 'Knock, and it shall be opened to you', and 'Seek and you shall find', but also: 'Ask, and it shall be given unto you'".[30]

[29] Cf. Ecumenical Council Vatican II, Dogmatic Constitution on Divine Revelation *Dei Verbum,* 25.

[30] Origen, *Epistola ad Gregorium*, 3: *PG* 11,92.

36. In personal prayer, each nun learns to be with the Lord (cf. *Mk.* 3:13; *Ps.* 37), she enjoys the grace of silence and solitude inhabited by the Divine Presence (cf. *Hos.* 2:16-17), she creates with the Lord Jesus a unique and authentic relationship finding meaning and joy in her consecration.[31]

The whole process is rooted in solitude and silence.[32] "Interior life demands the asceticism of time and body. It requires silence as a dimension to dwell in. It invokes solitude as an essential moment of purification and personal integration. It calls for hidden prayer to meet the Lord who lives in the secret, and to make of the heart the interior cell (cf. *Matt.* 6:6). The very personal and sacred place in which to wor-

[31] Cf. FRANCIS, *Apostolic Letter* to all consecracted people on the occasion of the Year of Consecrated life, (November 21, 2014), II, 1.

[32] CONGREGATION FOR INSTITUES OF CONSECRATED LIFE AND SOCIETIES OF APOSTOLIC LIFE, Directives on formation in Religious Institutes *Potissimum Institutioni*, Rome, (February 2, 1990), 38. Cf. FRANCIS, Ap. Const. *Vultum Dei quaerere*, (June 29, 2016), I, 33.

ship: *Let my Beloved come into his garden and let him taste its rarest fruits (Sg 4:16)".*[33]

37. Silence and solitude, places of encounter with God, the fruit of a human ascetic exercise, become a prophetic announcement. Times of greater solitude and withdrawal from daily rhythms are necessary to renew the reasons and joys of contemplative life and confirm the prophecy, as well as begin an inner journey that leads to the contemplation of God's Face.

Called to community

38. "The religious community has felt itself to be in continuity with the group of those who followed Jesus. He had called them personally, one by one, to live in communion with himself and with the other disciples, to share his life and his destiny (cf. *Mk.* 3:13-15), and in this to way to be a sign of the life and communion begun by him".[34]

[33] CONGREGATION FOR INSTITUES OF CONSECRATED LIFE AND SOCIETIES OF APOSTOLIC LIFE, *Contemplate. To consecrated men and women on the trail of Beauty,* LEV, Città del Vaticano 2015, 38.

[34] CONGREGATION FOR INSTITUES OF CONSECRATED LIFE AND SOCIETIES OF APOSTOLIC LIFE, *Fraternal Life in*

Within this vision, the life experience of sisters living in the monastery is the place of spiritual formation, the privileged place of communion with Christ, expression of the Church: "The first monastic communities looked to the community of the disciples who followed Christ and to the community of Jerusalem as being their ideal life. Like the nascent Church, having one heart and one soul, so the monks, gathering themselves under a spiritual guide, the abbot, set out to live the radical communion of material and spiritual goods and the unity established by Christ. This unity finds its archetype and its unifying dynamism in the life of unity of the Persons of the Most Blessed Trinity".[35]

39. The richness of the relationships of sisters within "an atmosphere of silence protected by the daily life of the cloister,"[36] accompanies the nun *in the vocation of universal sister in Christ*, with the tenderness of "Jesus our

Community. "Congregavit nos in unum Christi amor", (February 2, 1994), 10.

[35] *Ivi.*

[36] FRANCIS, Ap. Const. *Vultum Dei quaerere*, (June 29, 2016), 13.

Mother"[37], according to the intuition of Julian of Norwich. "Particularly significant is the witness offered by contemplative men and women. For them, fraternal life has broader and deeper dimensions which derive from the fundamental demand of this special vocation, the search for God alone in silence and prayer. Their constant attention to God makes their attention to other members of the community more delicate and respectful, and contemplation becomes a force liberating them from every form of selfishness. Fraternal life in common, in a monastery, is called to be a living sign of the mystery of the Church: the greater the mystery of grace, the richer the fruit of salvation".[38]

40. *It is indispensable* to form communities that share not only the same roof, liturgy and work, but also the same life: the experience of authentic humanity, a life of faith and prayer, living according to the Gospel and showing ex-

[37] Cf. Julian of Norwich, *Book of Showings,* Ancora, Milan 1984, 256 and 257.

[38] Congregation for Institues of consecrated life and Societies of apostolic life, *Fraternal Life in Community. "Congregavit nos in unum Christi amor",* (February 2, 1994), 10.

emplary solidarity (cf. *Matt.* 5:43-48; *Jn.* 13:34); fraternal help to the extreme consequences of the diakonia of love (cf. *Jn.* 15:13); personal and profound communication; enriching dialogue; friendly interrelations; a shared common plan that entails shared choices, the evaluation of paths and loving correction so that the means may always serve the common purpose. This welcoming sharing opens the way to hospitality and service to the poor, according to one's proper monastic charism.

In order to fulfil the above-mentioned goals, it is necessary to move from common life to communion of life, from the simple community to fraternal life in community.

In the fruitfulness of culture

41. Culture, a value always treasured by the monastic tradition, is a necessary formative factor for the human person and for spiritual and fraternal life.[39] Using the words of Pope Francis, the *four pillars* on which formation must

[39] Cf. Congregation for Institutes of consecrated life and Societies of apostolic life, Directives on formation in religious institutes *Potissimum Institutioni*, Rome, (February 2, 1990), 75.

be based, integrated with each other, include "study life"[40] for, as he reminds us, "grace supposes culture, and God's gift becomes flesh in the culture of those who receive it".[41]

Each community should establish an appropriate time for reading and personal study, supported by a "constantly updated library"[42] and documentation that can be accessed via the computer system. The help of people from outside the community,[43] experts and sisters from other monasteries may also be sought whenever necessary.

42. Formation should provide sound and balanced information embracing the whole of humanity, especially those who suffer. Contemplative sisters are called to inhabit history while cultivating an inner gaze. It is possible to con-

[40] FRANCIS, *The Strength of a Vocation. Consecrated Life Today*. Conversation with FERNANDO PRADO, 2, CCF, 2018, 78.

[41] FRANCIS, Ap. Ex. *Evangelii gaudium,* (November 24 2013), 115.

[42] CONGREGATION FOR INSTITUES OF CONSECRATED LIFE AND SOCIETIES OF APOSTOLIC LIFE, Directives on formation in religious institutes *Potissimum Institutioni*, Rome, (February 2, 1990), 84.

[43] Cf. *Ivi*, 82.

sult the press and digital communications media, with "prudent discernment aimed at ensuring that they remain truly at the service of formation to contemplative life"[44] and do not distract from a life hidden with Christ in God (cf. *Col.* 3:3). Information is not enough, it is necessary to read history through the intelligence of the heart; "the joys and the hopes, the griefs and the anxieties"[45] of all, assumed with the wisdom that comes from on high and with compassion.

The dignity of work

43. In formation to contemplative life, care should be given to education in manual and intellectual work, both as daily service to the life of the monastery and as a commitment and a contribution to the work carried out by the community for its own subsistence. In this way, each sister grows in the spirit of service, thereby maturing in her shared responsibility.[46]

[44] FRANCIS, Ap. Const. *Vultum Dei quaerere*, (June 29, 2016), 34.

[45] ECUMENICAL COUNCIL VATICAN II, Pastoral Constitution on the Church in the modern world *Gaudium et Spes*, 1.

[46] Cf. FRANCIS, Ap. Const. *Vultum Dei quaerere*, (June 29, 2016), 32.

44. Work also helps balancing the various aspects of life, an element of solidarity with all men and women, especially the poor, while keeping in mind the words of St. Benedict: "When they live by the labor of their hands, then they are really monks".[47] The evangelical message, the competence, the faithful commitment, the interior freedom, should permeate a sound conception and evaluation of labor to prevent it from becoming a temptation to ownership and a unique recognition of personal identity. Work must be carried out "with fidelity and devotion", without extinguishing "the spirit of prayer and devotion to which all other temporal things should be subordinated", in the words of the Poor Man of Assisi.[48]

In the mission of the Church according to the charism

45. Fidelity to the Spirit, which leads each charism to fruitfulness,[49] ensures the specif-

[47] BENEDICT, *Rule*, 48, 8.

[48] FRANCIS OF ASSISI, *Regula bullata*, V, 2-3; Cf. *Letter to St. Anthony*, 2.

[49] To ensure this fruitfulness, the founding charism, as Pope Francis attests, needs to be purified by restoring "the most authentic part of the foundational charisms

ic service of contemplative life in the Church and in the world, and thus being an "eloquent sign of communion, welcoming abodes for those seeking God and the things of the spirit, schools of faith and true places of study, dialogue and culture for the building up of the life of the Church and of the earthly city itself, in expectation of the heavenly city".[50]

46. Fidelity to the charism requires continuous formation in the sound ecclesiology of communion as envisaged by the Second Vatican Council. Deepening one's proper charismatic tradition must be placed in context and interpreted in the light of *sentire cum Ecclesia*, in harmony with the *sensus fidelium* and through intelligent discernment of the signs of the times. This formation is achieved through the study of Church Magisterium and of the formative

to see how this more authentic part is lived today [...]. Let us not turn them into museum pieces [...]. Today is the present, and that is where we have to respond from our charism [...]. Consecrated life is like water: if it is stagnat, it putrifies". FRANCIS, *The Strength of a Vocation. Consecrated Life Today*. Conversation with FERNANDO PRADO, 2, CCF, 2018, 1, 42-43. 45.

[50] JOHN PAUL II, Post-Synodal Ap. Ex. *Vita Consecrata,* (March 25, 1996), 6.

and legal literature elaborated by one's *Order* or by the Monastic Federation.

47. In this ecclesial perspective, every aspect of formation will be put in practice according to the original inspiration of one's Institute.[51] The formation process thus offers the individual guidance for the development of a vital synthesis of the charism, in order to live its spirit in cordial discernment with the monastic community, in harmony with the Church and the world today.

In this respect, in vocational accompaniment, starting with initial formation, a sincere feeling of heartfelt belonging to the Church should be cultivated: "...the path of consecrated life is the path of inclusion in the Church [...]. Thus we are talking about an ecclesial inclusion with ecclesial categories, with an ecclesial spiritual life [...]. There is no room for anything else".[52]

48. The charismatic patrimony manifests a twofold dynamism: its faithful transmission

[51] Cf. *Ivi*, 71.

[52] FRANCIS, *The Strength of a Vocation. Consecrated Life Today.* Conversation with FERNANDO PRADO, 2, CCF, 2018, 1, 41.

by the older nuns and its fruitful reception by the younger ones. Enhancing the experience of community life and interpreting its modes and practices, translating it into the language and symbolism of younger generations, is a necessary and fruitful process.

49. As a result of its autonomy, each monastery develops its inherent historical and spiritual distinctiveness, linked to the surrounding environment. An in-depth study of history and the specific vocation is appropriate in order to preserve its knowledge, while ensuring it is not *an exercise in archaeology.*[53]

The ecumenical vision

50. The Church encourages monastic life to be particularly receptive to ecumenism as a dimension of formation with a view to unification, ecclesial communion and compassion: "I entrust to the monasteries of contemplative life the spiritual ecumenism of prayer, conversion of heart, and charity. To this end I encourage their presence wherever Christian commu-

[53] Cf. FRANCIS, *Apostolic letter* to all Consecrated people on the occasion of the Year of Consecrated Life, (November 21, 2014), I, 1.

nities of different confessions live side by side, so that their total devotion to the *one thing needful* (cf. *Lk.* 10:42) – to the worship of God and to intercession for the salvation of the world, together with their witness of evangelical life according to their special charisms – will inspire everyone to abide, after the image of the Trinity, in that unity which Jesus willed and asked of the Father for all his disciples."[54]

Formative environment and agents of formation

51. The obedience of faith, *lectio divina*, intellectual commitment and study, liturgy, asceticism, *communitas*, the seriousness of work, rooted in fruitful silence, create and nourish an environment of formation leading to learning the spiritual art of seeking the Face of God.[55] Seeds of life capable of blossoming in love of contemplation of the Truth are thus planted.

This experience lived inside the walls of the cloister, seemingly outside of the world, becomes a place of prophetic sharing: "you

[54] John Paul II, Post-Synodal Ap. Ex. *Vita Consecrata,* (March, 25 1996), 101.

[55] Cf. Benedict, *Rule*, IV, 75.

are the voice of the Church as she ceaselessly praises, thanks, implores and intercedes for all mankind".[56]

52. The individual sister, the community, the Major Superior of the monastery, the formators, the President of the Federation and any experts are all agents of ongoing and initial formation for monastic life.[57]

53. They are all called to serve within the limits of their competence, in a spirit of intelligent and full collaboration – in harmony with the teachings of the Church Magisterium, with due consideration of contemporary cultures and the specific vocation to contemplative life – to ensure continuous and fruitful formation to the monastic *corpus*.

54. Moreover, the discernment of candidates should be the object of utmost atten-

[56] FRANCIS, Ap. Const. *Vultum Dei quaerere*, (June 29, 2016), 9.

[57] Cf. CONGREGATION FOR INSTITUTES OF CONSECRATED LIFE AND SOCIETIES OF APOSTOLIC LIFE, *Cor Orans.* Implementing instruction on women's contemplative life, (April 1, 2018), 237-241.

tion on the part of everyone to ensure they are "psychologically and affectively healthy".[58]

The individual sister

55. Under the action of the Holy Spirit, sisters in initial or continuous formation are the main protagonists of their formation, and as such they should assume with great responsibility the task that befits them as leading players in the life-long project of conversion and growth.[59]

56. Along this journey, each sister should show her availability to be accompanied by the interventions that the Lord, through the community, makes available, and to share her joys,

[58] Francis, *The Strength of a Vocation. Consecrated Life Today.* Conversation with Fernando Prado, 2, CCF, 2018, 81. The Pope places great emphasis on "great care for maturity, both human and affective", and "discerning with seriousness and also listening to the voice of experience that the Church has". He concludes: "When discernment is not taken seriously in all this, problems grow", *Ivi*, 82.

[59] Cf. Congregation for Institutes of consecrated life and Societies of apostolic life, *Cor Orans.* Implementing instruction on women's contemplative life, (April 1, 2018), 227.

hopes and concerns, thereby showing a great availability for formation with a view to discovering the self, being freed from self and becoming a new woman, free in heart.

The formator

57. Sisters who have been entrusted with a specific responsibility for formation should accept this task in a spirit of joyful service to the sisters. They should manifest the joy of their contemplative vocation and be committed to their personal formation.

58. The formators must have a profound experience of God through prayer, a wisdom coming from attentive listening to the Word of God, and a deep love for the spiritual realities of their proper charism, so as to accompany others on this journey.[60]

59. Formators must be fully aware that they are only *mediators* between God, the only true Formator, and those in formation, who are primarily responsible for their formation, thereby preventing all forms of dependence, helping

[60] Cf. John Paul II, Post-Synodal Ap. Ex. *Vita Consecrata,* (March 25, 1996), 66.

the sisters in formation to know themselves, with their possibilities and limits, to progress from sincerity to truth, and to properly resolve their difficulties. In this service, the formator should remember that her mission is to support and to sustain "insofar as possible".[61] It is a matter of "forming young people without pushing the limits".[62]

60. In addition to being transparent and consistent in their lives, formators have a special role in accompanying candidates and discerning the authenticity of God's calling to contemplative life, as well as the mission of transmitting to the persons entrusted to them "the beauty of following Christ and the value of the charism by which this is accomplished"[63]. They must thus have special regard for the following aptitudes:

- ability to listen, dialogue and self-giving;

[61] FRANCIS, *The Strength of a Vocation. Consecrated Life Today.* Conversation with FERNANDO PRADO, 2, CCF, 2018, 80.

[62] *Ivi*, 81.

[63] Cf. JOHN PAUL II, Post-Synodal Ap. Ex. *Vita Consecrata,* (March 25, 1996), 66.

- serene and objective knowledge of oneself, of personal limits and possibilities,
- emotional stability, ability to overcome frustration, to confidently express personal feelings and beliefs;
- human qualities of discernment, balance, serenity, patience, understanding, spirit of joy and genuine affection for the sisters entrusted to them.[64]

61. Careful discernment in their choice and special care in their formation is required for a formator: "We must always keep in mind that formation cannot be improvised and that it demands remote and continuous preparation. Without a solid formation of the formators, the prepared and trustworthy brothers and sisters of this ministry would not be able to provide the youngest members with real and promising accompaniment".[65]

[64] Cf. Francis, *The Strength of a Vocation. Consecrated Life Today*. Conversation with Fernando Prado, 2, CCF, 2018, 74ss.

[65] Cf. Congregation for Institues of consecrated life and Societies of apostolic life, *New wines in new wineskins*. The consecrated life and its ongoing challenges since Vatican II. Guidelines, 16.

62. Formators should dedicate enough time to prioritise their service. All other activities must be compatible with their main duty. In addition, it should always be remembered that personal dialogue, "a practice of irreplaceable and proven effectiveness",[66] is the chief instrument in the dynamics inherent in personalized formation, which is based on mutual trust.

63. This implies, on the part of the formator: earning this trust through patient listening, the absence of judgment, devoting sufficient time to the encounter, frequent dialogue, the ability to take on the tensions of the other, sincerity and humility in offering personal interpretations of what the sister is experiencing, discretion on what is confided to her, her personal coherence of life.

The Major Superior

64. The Major Superior, abbess, prioress, or president of a monastic Congregation, while attending to her own formation, should assume her role as formator of the sisters entrusted to

[66] Cf. JOHN PAUL II, Post-Synodal Ap. Ex. *Vita Consecrata,* (March 25, 1996), 66.

her with great responsibility. In these capacities she should:

- be attentive to the human and spiritual needs of those she serves;
- possess the human qualities of discernment, balance and respect for the gifts bestowed by the Lord upon each sister;
- live out and forge bonds of familiarity, trust, freedom and responsibility with all the sisters; value and manifest her love for them with simple human gestures;
- cultivate an attitude of dialogue, understood as a true and profound profession of faith. In this environment, her task is to foster the development of the community project of life, with the participation of all the nuns[67];
- build a community that is a genuinely privileged space for ongoing and initial formation; a community in which obedience is transformed into collaboration, poverty into solidarity, chastity into a means that opens the heart to

[67] Cf. JOHN PAUL II, Ap. Letter *Novo millennio ineunte,* (January 6, 2001), 45; CONGREGATION FOR INSTITUES OF CONSECRATED LIFE AND SOCIETIES OF APOSTOLIC LIFE, *New wines in new wineskins.* The consecrated life and its ongoing challenges since Vatican II. Guidelines, 20.

welcome others and to universal brotherhood; a community where prayer and all that each one carries within are cultivated, feelings in need of support; a community where one lives *the mysticism of the encounter, the mystique of living together.*[68]

65. The Superiors should rely more on example than on words in carrying out the task of helping the sisters in their integral growth and in being ever more conformed to the image of Christ. They should always remember that the Lord came not to be served but to serve (cf. *Matt.* 20:28).[69] As the Gospel is demanding, she too will have to be demanding for the essential, while being comprehensive with the sisters entrusted to her guidance, *without pushing the limits of their wounds.*[70]

[68] Cf. FRANCIS, *Apostolic letter* to all consecrated people on the occasion of the year of consecrated life, (November 21, 2014), II, 3.

[69] Cf. CONGREGATION FOR INSTITUES OF CONSECRATED LIFE AND SOCIETIES OF APOSTOLIC LIFE, *New wines in new wineskins.* The consecrated life and its ongoing challenges since Vatican II. Guidelines, 21.

[70] Cf. FRANCIS, *The Strength of a Vocation. Consecrated Life Today.* Conversation with FERNANDO PRADO, 2, CCF, 2018, 60.

The community

66. The nun learns how to be and become a contemplative sister inside the community and through daily participation in the life of a specific community and fraternity. The community is the place where the spirit of the founder/ foundress is a living reality; where the charism and the spirit are effectively lived and become manifest. The community is the physical and theological place where "initiation into the fatigue and joys of community life takes place".[71] "This requires the harmonious and appropriate collaboration and participation of the entire community"[72], with clear distinctions as well as complementarity of roles.

67. The involvement of the entire community in ongoing and initial formation means that each monastery should joyfully assume its formative role and fulfil the following necessary conditions to be truly such:

[71] Cf. John Paul II, Post-Synodal Ap. Ex. *Vita Consecrata,* (March 25 1996), 67.

[72] Congregation for Institutes of consecrated life and Societies of apostolic life, *New wines in new wineskins.* The consecrated life and its ongoing challenges since Vatican II. Guidelines, 16.

- quality of fraternal of life marked by an atmosphere of trust, dialogue and kindness that fosters liturgical and personal prayer, listening to the Word of God, studying and working;
- general coherence of explicit and implicit educational messages and the reality of consecrated life;
- expressing the beauty of contemplative life, fully consecrated to the Lord;
- having the ability to challenge in the calling to go beyond;
- having the willingness to grow together and establish a formative relationship among its members, especially with candidates undergoing formation;
- a sense of responsibility towards the community on the part of the sisters who form part of it;
- a project of fraternal life, the fruit of community discernment, which respects and values diversity as a richness, cooperation between the young and the older sisters, understanding for those who make mistakes and have not yet learned;
- willingness to deal with conflicts and to seek a solution together, with the help

of experts if needed, to ensure that the community is a privileged place for ongoing conversion;

– awareness of history and openness to the poor and the marginalized in harmony with the personal choice of contemplative life.

The Federal President

68. The Federal President and her Federal Council, in close cooperation with the Major Superiors, promotes and coördinates formation at the federal level; organises permanent formation activities for the Major Superiors and the formators of the Federation[73].

69. The Federal President, with her Council, elaborates the *Ratio Formationis* of the Federation, in conformity with this *Ratio*, ensuring an integral, organic, gradual and coherent formation for the sisters of the Federation.[74] The

[73] Cf. CONGREGATION FOR INSTITUES OF CONSECRATED LIFE AND SOCIETIES OF APOSTOLIC LIFE, *Cor orans.* Implementing instruction on women's contemplative life, (April 1, 2018), 117-120.

[74] Cf. *Ivi*, 225. 226.

Ratio must be approved by the Federal Assembly in order to come into force.

Resorting to experts

70. If necessary, psycho-pedagogical sciences may be employed in personalised accompaniment, in order to support the development of a balanced personality as well as passing through some delicate stages of life. This should be done keeping in mind that the service of accompaniment does not replace the work of God, the first and only Formator and accompanier, nor the work of those who are accompanied, who have the primary responsibility for their own formation.

Ongoing formation

Ratio formationis

71. As repeatedly affirmed, formation is a process whereby it is the individual religious who is primarily responsible.[1] In this vision, the word of the Apostle resonates: *For this reason I remind you to fan into flame the gift of God, which is in you* (*2Tm* 1:6). In particular, the Code of Canon Law expresses this unavoidable process when it states: "After first profession, the formation of all members in each Institute is to be completed, so that they may lead the life proper to the Institute more fully, and fulfil its mission more effectively" (Can. 659).

72. The drafting of a proper *Ratio formationis* remains a path yet to be followed by many Federations. "The *Ratio* responds to a pressing need today. On the one hand, it shows how to pass on the Institute's spirit so that it will be

[1] Cf. FRANCIS, Cost. Ap. *Vultum Dei quaerere*, (June 29, 2016), 13.

lived in its integrity by future generations, in different cultures and geographical regions; on the other hand, it explains to consecrated persons how to live that spirit in the different stages of life on the way to the full maturity of faith in Christ.

While it is true that the renewal of consecrated life depends primarily on formation, it is equally certain that this formation is, in turn, linked to the ability to establish a method characterized by spiritual and pedagogical wisdom, gradually leading those who wish to consecrate themselves to take on the feelings of Christ the Lord".[2]

73. The *Ratio formationis* is thus a formation proposal for women called to live out the *sequela Christi* in contemplative life: "From the beginning of Christ's mission, women show a special sensitivity to him and to his mystery which is characteristic of their femininity".[3] This inherent attitude of consecrated women is a "*sign of God's tender love towards the human race* and a

[2] John Paul II, Post-Synodal Ap. Ex. *Vita Consecrata,* (March 25, 1996), 68.

[3] John Paul II, *Mulieris dignitatem*, (August 15, 1988), 16.

special witness to the mystery of the Church, Virgin, Bride and Mother".[4]

74. It will be drawn up at the federal level and applied to all the monasteries as a primary and indispensable project, thereby ensuring a genuine path of formation.[5]

Formation of nuns

75. The purpose of consecrated life is conformity to the Lord Jesus and to his *total oblation*, whereby formation initiates and accompanies this itinerary of progressive *assimilation of Christ's feelings to the Father*. The formative method "should include and express the *character of wholeness*. Formation should involve the whole person, in every aspect of the personality, in behaviour and intentions. Precisely because it aims at the transformation of the whole person, it is clear that *the formative commitment never ends*".[6]

[4] JOHN PAUL II, Post-Synodal Ap. Ex. *Vita Consecrata*, (March 25, 1996), 57.

[5] *Ivi*, 68.

[6] *Ivi*, 65.

76. "Permanent formation, whether in Institutes of apostolic or contemplative life, is an intrinsic requirement of religious consecration [...]. *Initial formation*, then, should be closely connected with *permanent* formation, thereby creating a readiness on everyone's part to let oneself be formed every day of one's life".[7] Ongoing formation thus coincides with ascetic commitment in the broadest sense of the term and it lasts forever.[8] "In order to ensure adequate ongoing formation, federations are to promote cooperation between monasteries through the exchange of formative materials and the use of digital means of communication, always exercising due discretion".[9]

The monastic community: mystical encounter

77. "The ordinary place where the formative process takes place is the monastery".[10] The

[7] *Ivi*, 69.

[8] Cf. Congregation for Institues of consecrated life and Societies of apostolic life, *Cor orans.* Implementing instruction on women's contemplative life, (April 1, 2018), 231ff.

[9] Cf. Francis, Ap. Const. *Vultum Dei querere*, (June 29, 2016), Conclusion and regulations, art. 3 §2.

[10] *Ivi*, I, 14.

monastic community adheres to the mystery of communion and it "seeks to reflect the depth and richness of this mystery, taking shape as a human community in which the Trinity dwells, in order to extend in history the gifts of communion proper to the three divine Persons".[11]

Therefore with this vision, the community should devote special attention to ongoing formation, "*the foundation* of every stage of formation".[12] Authenticity of life has thus to be preserved, in dynamic fidelity to one's proper charism, in the awareness that monastic witness constitutes the first and eloquent vocational proclamation.

78. Monastic formation, of a fundamentally communitarian nature, accompanies the experience of fraternal communion, a "*God-enlightened space* in which to experience the hidden presence of the risen Lord (cf. *Matt.* 18:20)[13]. This happens thanks to the mutual love of all the members of the community, a love which is

[11] John Paul II, Post-Synodal Ap. Ex. *Vita consecrata,* (March 25, 1996), 41.

[12] Francis, Ap. Const. *Vultum Dei querere*, (June 29, 2016), Conclusion and regulations, art.3 §1

[13] *Ivi*, 42.

nourished by the Word and the Eucharist, purified in the Sacrament of Reconciliation, and sustained by prayer for unity, the special gift of the Spirit to those who obediently listen to the Gospel. It is the Spirit himself who leads the soul to the experience of communion with the Father and with his Son Jesus Christ (cf. *1 Jn.* 1:3), a communion which is the source of fraternal life".[14]

79. The monastic community is "the place and the natural setting of the process of growth, where everyone is co-responsible for the growth of others".[15] Rich in spiritual gifts, it provides guidance in following the Lord Jesus. In it "each one learns to live with those whom God has put at his or her side, accepting their positive traits along with their differences and limitations. Each one learns to share the gifts received for the building up of all, because *to*

[14] JOHN PAUL II, Post-Synodal Ap. Ex. *Vita consecrata,* (March 25, 1996), 42

[15] CONGREGATION FOR INSTITUES OF CONSECRATED LIFE AND SOCIETIES OF APOSTOLIC LIFE, *Fraternal life in the community. "Congregavit nos in unum Christi amor",* (February 2, 1994), 43.

each is given the manifestation of the Spirit for the common good (1 Cor. 12:7)".[16]

80. For this reason, each opportunity to get to know one another, to share spiritual goods and to grow in one's sense of belonging[17] must be practiced, because "no one contributes to the future in isolation, by his or her efforts alone, but by seeing himself or herself as part of a true communion which is constantly open to encounter, dialogue, attentive listening and mutual assistance".[18] It should also be remembered that "by constantly promoting fraternal love, also in the form of common life, the consecrated life has shown that *participating in the Trinitarian communion can change human relationships* and create a new type of solidarity".[19]

[16] Cf. JOHN PAUL II, Post-Synodal Ap. Ex. *Vita consecrata,* (March 25, 1996), 67.

[17] Cf. CONGREGATION FOR INSTITUES OF CONSECRATED LIFE AND SOCIETIES OF APOSTOLIC LIFE, *Starting Afresh from Christ: A renewed commitment to consecrated life in the Third Millennium*, (May 19, 2002), 28.

[18] Cf. FRANCIS, *Apostolic Letter* to all consecrated persons on the occasion of the Year of Consecrated Life, (November 21, 2014), II, 3.

[19] Cf. JOHN PAUL II, Post-Synodal Ap. Ex. *Vita consecrata,* (March 25, 1996), 41.

The lack of communication and sharing results in a weakening of fraternity while the spiritual experience acquires an individualistic connotation[20] that may deplete the life of individuals and community alike.

81. "One of the challenges which is particularly felt today is to integrate members who were given a different formation [...] into one single community life, in such a way that these differences become not so much occasions of conflict but moments of mutual enrichment".[21] Each consecrated person, with her own talents, witness, personal story, is called to confront herself with the community in order to experience relationships whereby the communion among sisters is for the world *confessio trinitatis:* the beauty and the living grace of participation in the divine communion.[22]

[20] Cf. CONGREGATION FOR INSTITUES OF CONSECRATED LIFE AND SOCIETIES OF APOSTOLIC LIFE, *Fraternal Life in Community. "Congregavit nos in unum Christi amor"*, (February 2,1994), 31.

[21] *Ivi*, 43.

[22] Cf. *Ivi*, 24-27.

Generating Christ in the disciples

82. "God the Father, through the unceasing gift of Christ and the Spirit, is the formator par excellence of those who consecrate themselves to him. But in this work, he makes use of human mediation, placing more mature brothers and sisters at the side of those whom he calls".[23] Formation of nuns is the responsibility of the monastic community governed and animated by the Major Superior of the monastery, with the support of her assistants.

83. The tradition of monasticism clearly testifies to the recognition that the primary objective of those responsible for the communion in the monastery is to *generate Christ in the disciples* (cf. 2 *Cor.* 3:18), looking "for paths and for solidity, in other words, for the maturity of consecration. A consecrated person cannot be like a child. She must be an adult".[24]

[23] John Paul II, Post-Synodal Ap. Ex. *Vita consecrata,* (March 25, 1996), 66.

[24] Francis, *The Strength of a Vocation. Consecrated Life Today.* Conversation with Fernando Prado, CCF, 2018, 2, 53.

84. Furthermore, the Superior accompanies the sisters on the path of formation according to the *Rule*, a path of intelligence, a path of the heart that is never formal, sustaining the freedom of the person, who gradually learns to open herself up to the surprise of the other and to trust in mediation, while she assimilates the filial feelings of Christ the Lord into her being and her actions.

85. This *traditio* offers a formative opportunity which, through living and continuous hermeneutics, is able to express the identity of the service of authority according to the charism of each Order. This interpretative process makes it possible to draw on the original inspiration of the *Rule* in a new spirit, whatever the style, history, observances and activities characterising the life of the monastery. The community thus chooses the Superior in order to be edified and guided along the path of her vocation and ongoing formation according to the proper charism.

86. The path of ongoing formation should be pursued with an open spirit of cooperation and *synodality*. The Superior shall respect and cultivate these indispensable principles in her relationship with the nuns, the formators, the federal President, the authorities of the Church, in order for the path to be vital, wise and capable of engendering a full life.

Multicultural integration

87. While "the recruitment of candidates from other countries solely for the sake of ensuring the survival of a monastery is to be absolutely avoided",[25] the reception of young vocations coming from other Countries and cultures which are different from that of the monastery will entail their gradual formation, aimed at integration into the religious community. They shall thereby experience in full their female monastic identity, taking on its responsibilities in a process of growth and cultural integration that will bring their freedom to maturity. The knowledge of cultural and social conditions, problems and expectations characterising the origins of candidates from other countries needing initiation into monastic life is a precondition for starting and proceeding along the path of formation.

[25] Cf. FRANCIS, Ap. Const. *Vultum Dei querere*, (June 29, 2016), Conclusion and regulations, art. 3 §6.

Special periods

88. Special periods for formation have to be planned during the year by the Federal President, upon consultation with the Superiors of the federated monasteries. In the event of internal resources declining – in the monastery as well as in a monastic federation – mutual assistance is recommended, even among different Orders, to ensure effective support in ongoing formation.

89. In periods of transition, typical of the different stages of life, special attention must be paid to the formation of every nun. In particular: in the disillusion experienced after perpetual profession; in mid-life, when one pauses to evaluate the meaning and fruitfulness of one's existence; in times of fragility, of limitations, of discouragement, of intensification of internal processes that demand clarity in discernment and audacity in decisions. "Therefore, it will be the responsibility of persons in authority to keep a high level of formative availability as well as the ability to learn from life, the freedom of letting oneself be formed by others and for each one to feel a responsibility for the growth of others".[26]

Formation of formators

90. Those in charge of formation "must therefore be very familiar with the path of seeking God, so as to be able to accompany others on this journey. Sensitive to the action of grace, they will also be able to point out those obstacles which are less obvious. But above all they will disclose the beauty of following Christ and the value of the charism by which this is accomplished. They will combine the illumination of spiritual wisdom with the light shed by human means, which can help both in discerning the call and in forming the new man or woman, until they are genuinely free".[27]

91. Since "a person's growth is always hand-crafted", it is essential that the formators

[26] CONGREGATION FOR INSTITUES OF CONSECRATED LIFE AND SOCIETIES OF APOSTOLIC LIFE, Instruction *The service of authority and obedience. Faciem tuam, Domine, requiram,* (May 11, 2008),13g.

[27] JOHN PAUL II, Post-Synodal Ap. Ex. *Vita consecrata,* (March 25, 1996), 66.

are "women of discernment, of intense religiosity and patience", so as to *accompany the person*, valuing her as she is, *in order to accompany her, little by little, according to the principles of the charism.*[28]

92. Special attention will be given to the selection of sisters to serve as formators in the accompaniment of candidates along the path of initial formation and in ensuring cooperation with the Superior of the monastery so that the monastic community may live a fruitful environment of ongoing formation, proceeding in harmony with the daily requirements of contemplative life.[29]

93. Individual monasteries and federations are to make every effort to ensure a sound preparation of formators and their assistants. Sisters charged with the "sensitive task of formation may also attend, *servatis de iure servandis*, specific courses on formation outside their monastery".[30]

[28] FRANCIS, *The Strength of a Vocation. Consecrated Life Today.* Conversation with FERNANDO PRADO, CCF, 2018, 2, 74-76.

[29] Cf. FRANCIS, Ap. Const. *Vultum Dei querere*, (June 29, 2016), Conclusion and regulations, art. 3 § 3-4.

[30] *Ivi*, Conclusion and regulations, art. 3 § 4.

94. It will be the task of the Federal Superior to make such decisions with careful discernment, ensuring that the attendance does not separate the sisters from the life of the monastery for a timeframe exceeding seven days in the course of a month, in an "environment always fitting and consistent with the needs of their own charism".[31]

Formation of superiors

95. Monastic communities must be guided with loving and intelligent wisdom, in the style of Christ: *I am among you as the one who serves* (*Lk.* 22:27). "In consecrated life, authority is first of all a spiritual authority. Persons in authority recognize that they are called to serve an ideal that is much greater than themselves, an ideal which can be approached only in an atmosphere of prayer and humble seeking, which allows them to grasp the action of the same Spirit in the heart of every brother or sister".[32]

[31] FRANCIS, Ap. Const. *Vultum Dei querere*, (June 29, 2016), Conclusion and regulations, art. 3 § 4.

[32] CONGREGATION FOR INSTITUES OF CONSECRATED LIFE AND SOCIETIES OF APOSTOLIC LIFE, Instruction *The*

96. "Persons called to exercise authority must know that they will be able to do so only if they first undertake the pilgrimage leading to seeking God's will with intensity and righteousness".[33] Those called to carry out the service of authority must be attentive to their own formation.[34] Such formation should be based on the Church Magisterium; on a pedagogy of the human person; on a specific knowledge of contemporary signs and cultures. "To be in the position of promoting the spiritual life, persons in authority will have to cultivate first in themselves an openness to listening to others and to the signs of the times through a daily familiarity in prayer with the Word of God, with the Rule and the other norms of the life".[35]

97. Formation of Superiors should not neglect the importance of an authoritative and

service of authority and obedience. Faciem tuam, Domine, requiram, (May 11, 2008), 13a.

[33] *Ivi*, 12.

[34] Francis, Ap. Const. *Vultum Dei querere*, (June 29, 2016), Conclusion and regulations, art. 7 § 1.

[35] Congregation for Institues of consecrated life and Societies of apostolic life, Instruction *The service of authority and obedience. Faciem tuam, Domine, requiram*, (May 11, 2008), 13 a.

maternal presence accompanying the life of the sisters: "The service of authority demands a constant presence, able to enliven and take initiative, to recall the raison d'être of consecrated life, to help the persons to correspond with ever-renewed fidelity to the call of the Spirit".[36]

Formation of treasurers

98. The economic dimension of monastic communities must be managed with utmost wisdom, care and expertise, especially in cases involving the management of considerable assets. Hence adequate preparation is necessary for the sisters in charge of administration.[37]

The temporal goods of religious institutes are ecclesiastical goods (can. 635 § 1). All temporal goods which belong to public legal entities in the Church are ecclesiastical goods (can. 1257 § 1), directed to a purpose befitting the Church's mission (can. 114 § 1). In fact, the goods of institutes "serve the same evangelical

[36] *Ivi.*

[37] Congregation for Instititues of consecrated life and Societies of apostolic life, *Economy at the service of the Charism and Mission. Boni dispensatores multiformis gratiae Dei. Guidelines*, LEV (2018), 18-19.

purpose of promoting the human person, the mission, and charitable and supportive sharing with the people of God. A common commitment to the concern and care for the poor can give new vitality to an Institute".[38]

99. It should be remembered that "through finances, vital choices are made which should reflect the evangelical witness, always mindful of the needs of our brothers and sisters. The evangelical dimension of our finances should not therefore be neglected in the formative process, especially in the formation of those who will have to manage economic structures following the principles of gratuitousness, fraternity and justice, laying the foundations for evangelical economics of sharing and communion (cf. *Acts* 4:32-35)".[39]

[38] Congregation for Institutes of consecrated life and Societies of apostolic life, *New wines in new wineskins. The consecrated life and its ongoing challenges since Vatican II.* Guidelines, Rome, (January 6, 2017), 28.

[39] Congregation for Institutes of consecrated life and Societies of apostolic life, Circ. lett. *Guidelines for the Administration of the Assets in Institutes of Consecrated Life and Societies of Apostolic life*, (August 2, 2014), 4.

The Ordinary formative plan

Personal and communal

100. Each sister elaborates a *personal formative plan* concerning her life of following Christ; the monastic Chapter elaborates a *plan of community life* regarding formation in the monastic community.[40] The *plan of community life* based on the *Rule* and periodically updated lays down an adequate formation programme. Each member should be able to participate in the community's formation programme and have the opportunity for personal reflection.

The Federal formative plan

101. The Federal President, with her proper Council and the participation of the Superiors of the respective monasteries should draft a Federal formative plan in accordance with the principles and criteria of the *Ratio formationis*. It should set out specific periods and areas of formation: for formators for contemplative life; for the professed in temporary vows; for

[40] FRANCIS, Ap. Const. *Vultum Dei querere,* (June 29 2016), Conclusion and regulations, art. 3 § 1.

the nuns of the monasteries of the Federation; for the superiors and the treasurers. The periods and methods for the process of initial formation should also be verified.

For the formators

102. The formators must therefore be very familiar with the path of seeking God, so as to be able to accompany others on this journey. Sensitive to the action of grace, they will disclose the beauty of following Christ and the value of the charism by which this is accomplished, and they will also be able to point out those obstacles which are less obvious. Illuminated by spiritual wisdom, they will also use the tools of human science which can help both in discerning the call and "in forming the new man or woman, until they are genuinely free. The chief instrument of formation is personal dialogue, a practice of irreplaceable and commendable effectiveness which should take place regularly and with a certain frequency. Because sensitive tasks are involved, the formation of suitable formators, who will fulfil their task in a spirit of communion with the whole Church, is very important".[41]

[41] John Paul II, Post-Synodal Ap. Ex. *Vita consecrata,* (March 25, 1996), 66.

103. The formator should cultivate her firm belief that Christ is the true life (cf. *2 Cor* 5:14-17) and that her service is to introduce to the beauty of the new life, of the *life hidden with Christ in God* (*Col* 3:3). In this spirit, she will first educate herself to live according to the logic of the Paschal Mystery, *kenosis*, which transforms the human person into the new life of the Holy Spirit, and will receive the skill of discernment and grace in order to guide others on this demanding journey.

104. As for the formation of formators, it is recommended that the internal courses of the federation as well as the attendance of external Schools include adequate sessions for *ad hoc* formation that do not require spending excessively long periods of time outside the monastery. Appropriate places should be chosen so as to preserve an adequate and favourable environment.

For the temporary or simply professed sisters

105. Dedicated programmes for the formation of temporary professed sisters should be carried out with federal courses offering the possibility of specific formation along with valuable proposals of meetings and exchange of experiences among nuns from different monasteries. Planning a suitable formative period for immediate preparation to perpetual profession should also be envisaged.

For the perpetually or solemn professed

106. In order to ensure ongoing formation of perpetually professed religious, the Federal President is to promote cooperation among monasteries through the exchange of formative materials and the use of digital means of communication,[42] or by offering targeted formation courses, open to the participation of the communities of the Federation and/or the Confederation.

Cultural domains

107. We shall hereby point out some inspirational, non-exhaustive cultural domains that should be considered as reference in programmes for the ongoing and initial formation of contemplatives: *Exegesis* of Scripture; *Sacred Liturgy* and *Sacred Music; Patristic Literature; Monastic Literature* including the charismatic sourc-

[42] Francis, Ap. Const. *Vultum Dei querere*, (June 29, 2016), Conclusion and regulations, Art. 3 § 2.

es of the Institute; *Theological and anthropological spiritual literature; Magisterium of the Second Vatican Council; Ecclesial Magisterium,* especially on consecrated life; *Humanistic and pedagogical Literature; Iconic Art.* Other domains of special interest (botanical, pharmaceutical, editorial, confectionery, etc.) may serve to harmonize study and work.

In a digital culture

108. Special formative care should ensure that nuns have prudent access to digital culture: "These media can prove helpful for formation and communication. At the same time, I urge – states Pope Francis – a prudent discernment aimed at ensuring that they remain truly at the service of formation to contemplative life and necessary communication".[43]

109. It is not simply a question of using communication media or prohibiting their use, with prior discernment of the Superior who entrusts a nun with the management of digital *media.* In fact, this involves understanding the languages, the symbols as well as the complex

[43] *Ivi*, 34.

and often manipulative methods found in the media culture through dedicated formation. Online information can be a formative means only if one is familiar with the nature of such means of communication – completely different from oral or written communication.

110. In monastic life, it is necessary to keep proper distance from the continuous flow of information in order to avoid redundant emotional impact. Therefore, a distinction should be made between *internet* access as a means of work, formation and information, and its use as a moment of leisure and relaxation. Particular attention should be paid to the cell, which should retain its distinctive feature of meditation and prayer.

111. Firstly, the media world concerns the methodology of study and critical reflection. It is necessary to help nuns not to give in to the fascination of immediate, easy and fluid fruition of the study subjects, which is not limited to the management of information without criteria for discernment and criticism.

112. As in other areas of life, uncontrolled management – as well as elitist and privileged management – is inappropriate when using the means of digital culture. Aside from practical and particular choices, it is important that a community has a defined set of criteria for using the *Internet.* It is a matter of initiating a process of maturation towards a shared style of use responding to the needs of contemplative life with respect to the time and place in which it can be used, as well as the amount of time allowed to each user.

113. The monastic Chapter has the duty to discern the amount of time and modalities regulating the access to information channels. The Superior and the formators, while avoiding a mere supervisory function, initiate processes of trust and instilling a sense of responsibility in each sister, inviting them to share their experience in the digital field.

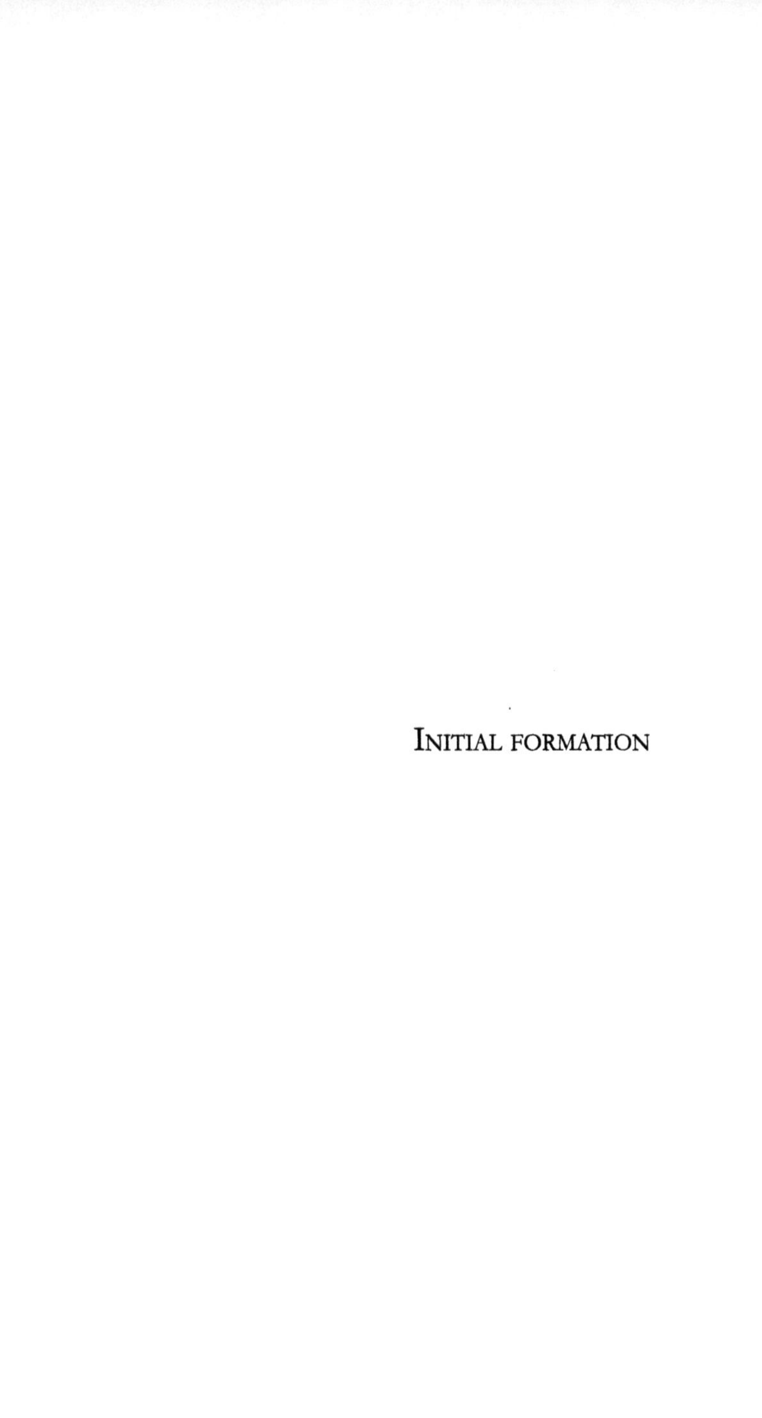

Initial formation

In contemporary cultural contexts

114. "Sufficient time should be reserved for initial formation, understood as a process of development which passes through every stage of personal maturity – from the psychological and spiritual to the theological and pastoral",[1] corresponding to no less than nine years and not more than twelve.[2]

115. Contemporary cultures, especially Western ones, have shaped a new human anthropology focusing on the autonomy of the person as an individual, highlighting spontaneity, fulfilment of every desire and self-realization. In other countries, in some cases, the legitimate desire for social emancipation may

[1] John Paul II, Post-synodal Ap. Ex. *Vita consecrata,* (March 25, 1996), 65.

[2] Congregation for Institutes of consecrated life and Societies of apostolic life, *Cor Orans.* Implementing instruction on women's contemplative life, (April 1, 2018), 253.

motivate the decision to begin a journey in religious communities. In both cases, it is increasingly complex to conceive and plan life in the oblative vision of oneself, especially when it involves a radical and definitive choice.

116. Women asking Institutes of Contemplative Life to enter into the dignity and requirements of this state of consecrated life must be accompanied in an appropriate and specific way. Monasteries, therefore, should employ sound pedagogy and humble mystagogy to introduce candidates to understanding the nature of life ordained to cloistered contemplation, along with the needs that support it.

117. Every woman undertaking the path of discipleship in monastic life has the duty to preserve a living desire for God, cultivating an intelligence of the heart that cannot be improvised and that must be nurtured with passion during the entire life. Therefore, in the daily journey, it is necessary to help the youngest ones not to succumb to the temptation of instant gratification.

118. In individual study and formation, it is necessary to grow accustomed to the effort of reflection and in-depth learning, thereby avoiding the illusion of a culture based on mere information. Native-digital youth accustomed to live online should be taught a calm and reflective way of managing information, that digs *down deep* (*Lk.* 6:48).

119. Such principles must be known and accepted by the candidates in the period of initial formation. The contemplatives "are placed in a state of personal oblation so high as to require a special vocation which must be verified before admission or final profession".[3]

Discernment and vocational confirmation

120. In the monastic *tradition*, founders and foundresses and their disciples were masters in the art of seeking God. In the Rule, St. Benedict states that the disposition to be sought in a novice is *si revera Deum quaerit.*[4] Discernment entails verifying the disposition to embrace a demanding lifestyle that requires renouncing one's own patterns and habits. Careful discern-

[3] JOHN PAUL II, *General Audience,* Rome, (January 4, 1995), 8.

[4] Cf. BENEDICT, *Rule,* 58,7, in FRANCIS, Ap. Const. *Vultum Dei querere,* (June 29, 2016), 2.

ment is required, therefore not being influenced by numbers or efficiency[5], but illuminated by the evangelical values characterising contemplative life.[6]

Promotion and vocational accompaniment

121. Every monastery ought to ensure that vocations are promoted, first of all through prayer, as an act of obedience to the Word "pray therefore the Lord of the harvest to send out labourers into his harvest" (*Lk.* 10:2), entrusting themselves to the Holy Spirit; paths of catechesis and proclamation should be created to offer young people a space for learning the charism, raising questions in their hearts and encouraging their answers.[7]

122. Sisters who are passionate about the charism and capable of entering in dialogue

[5] Cf. CONGREGATION FOR INSTITUTES OF CONSECRATED LIFEAND SOCIETIES OF APOSTOLIC LIFE, *Starting Afresh from Christ: A renewed commitment to consecrated life in the Third Millennium*, (May 19, 2002), 18.

[6] Cf. FRANCIS, Ap. Const. *Vultum Dei querere*, (June 29, 2016), 6.

[7] Cf. JOHN PAUL II, Post-synodal Ap. Ex. *Vita consecrata*, (March 25, 1996), 64.

with the youth of today and understanding their nature should be appropriately formed in vocational accompaniment. These sisters should commit themselves to a path of personal encounters where the young candidates are given the opportunity to engage with the charism in a more direct and personal way. In this phase, the young candidate is invited, when possible, to be a temporary guest of the monastery, in order to foster deeper mutual understanding.

The formation process

Aspirancy

123. The aptitude for oblative love overcomes the fatigue that lies at the heart of every new start and every transformation.[8] It is therefore necessary to wisely discern the docility of the heart and its docility to the Lord, to the circumstances and obstacles of life. The continuous struggle between the desire to follow Christ in monastic life and daily life experience requires choosing and persevering in the practical application of the Gospel.

[8] Cf. BENEDICT, *Rule,* Prologue, 48-49.

124. The young candidates who persevere in their intention to pursue the path after a proper stage of vocational discernment can be welcomed into the cloister for further verification in the context of the reality of daily life. They will be accompanied by the formator tasked with closely following their path. It is the responsibility of the monastic Chapter to determine the modalities and duration of this experience in the cloister, which will normally last one year, and may be eventually extended.

125. The Congregation for Institutes of Consecrated Life and Societies of Apostolic Life should be consulted when accepting candidates from abroad while scrupulously following the established procedure, taking into account that "even though the establishment of international and multicultural communities is a sign of the universality of the charism, the recruitment of candidates from other countries solely for the sake of ensuring the survival of a monastery is to be absolutely avoided".[9]

[9] Francis, Ap. Const. *Vultum Dei querere*, (June 29, 2016), Conclusion and regulations, Art. 3 § 6.

126. In this first phase, the *Ratio formationis* should incorporate acceptance criteria for candidates, supported by rigorous vocational discernment, taking into consideration the different ethnic and cultural backgrounds.

Postulancy

127. The purpose of postulancy is to accompany the process of discernment of the candidate prior to the candidate's admission into the novitiate, having ascertained a sufficient degree of human and religious maturity[10] and having initiated the necessary process of growth, to be perfected and deepened during the novitiate. This stage requires personalized paths, starting from human maturity and the preparation of each candidate. The process progresses through daily and serene accompaniment that fosters emotional and relational balance and the initiation into consecrated life.

128. The period of postulancy may not last less than one year and may be eventually

[10] Cf. CONGREGATION FOR INSTITUES OF CONSECRATED LIFE AND SOCIETIES OF APOSTOLIC LIFE, Directives on formation in religious institutes *Potissimum Institutioni*, Rome, (February 2, 1990), 42.

extended. In this stage of formation, the postulant should have the opportunity to verify whether she is able to fulfil the requirements of a contemplative life as proposed by the Church in the Apostolic Constitution *Vultum Dei quaerere* and, in particular, to establish a closer and more concrete relationship with the community with which she may decide to share her life.

Novitiate

129. The novitiate shall be carried out in accordance with universal law and may not last less than two years. The novitiate is a significant time in the path of initial formation, "a time of integral initiation into the form of life which the Son of God embraced and which he proposes to us in the Gospel".[11] This period should be treated with special care "in an atmosphere that is favourable to becoming deeply rooted in a life with Christ",[12] in the awareness that the novice bears within herself the human identity

[11] *Ivi*, 45.

[12] CONGREGATION FOR INSTITUES OF CONSECRATED LIFE AND SOCIETIES OF APOSTOLIC LIFE, Directives on formation in religious institutes *Potissimum Institutioni*, Rome, (February 2, 1990), 50.

of our time, marked by strong contradictions. The novitiate should hence be characterized by the identity of monastic life as a specific path of humanization and discipleship.

130. The novice learns "to say *yes* to the Lord's call by taking on the dynamism for maturing in one's vocation". It is an inescapable personal responsibility for it "opens one's whole life to the action of the Holy Spirit", going through the path of formation with generosity, "and accepting with faith the means of grace offered by the Lord and the Church. Formation should therefore have a profound effect on individuals, so that every attitude and action, at important moments as well as in the ordinary events of life, will show that they belong completely and joyfully to God".[13]

Period of temporary profession

131. This period, carried out in accordance with universal law, shall not last less than five years. As it precedes definitive profession, this time must be planned in such a way as to enable the professed members to be fully integrated

[13] John Paul II, Post-synodal Ap. Ex. *Vita consecrata,* (March 25, 1996), 65.

into the life of the community, that they may learn more about its gifts and limitations, and reach the stage of perpetual profession in full knowledge of the state of life and of the monastic community which they embrace forever.

132. Community life is a precious place to know oneself and one's gifts and enhance them in fraternal relationships. It should be remembered that the years of temporary profession are a period of formation, in which regular lessons, dialogues with formators, along with appropriate personal spaces for reflection and study, must be guaranteed.[14]

133. The young professed must be helped to arrange a proper balance between study and community commitment, life of prayer and generosity in service, solitude and fraternal relationships. This balance will be cherished during the entire course of their life.

134. In this stage of formation, the service to community life should not prevail. There-

[14] Cf. Congregation for Institues of consecrated life and Societies of apostolic life, Directives on formation in religious institutes *Potissimum Institutioni*, Rome, (February 2, 1990), 58.

fore, a specific programme should be provided for in the *Federal formative plan.*

Formation houses in the federation

135. It is advisable, given the importance of the formation process especially of the Novitiate, to promote common formation houses with a view to supporting those monasteries where the formation of the novices cannot be guaranteed.[15] The President and her Council are charged with the responsibility of establishing a common house of formation within the Federation, and of determining whether individual monasteries are in a position to ensure that the novitiate period progresses appropriately. Monasteries should always be granted the freedom to send their novices to any common formation house, even of a different Federation than the one they belong to.

Balance and harmony

136. In initial formation, the time reserved for work should not encroach upon that which

[15] Cf. FRANCIS, Ap. Const. *Vultum Dei quaerere*, (June 29, 2016), Conclusion and regulations, Art. 3 § 7.

is normally reserved for formation[16]: this attention should guide the regular organisation of monastic life.

137. Prior to perpetual profession, the professed will experience a period of intense preparation, during which they will be relieved of their usual occupations. The modalities of this preparation are laid down in the *Federal formative plan.*

Areas of formation

138. This multidisciplinary process – which integrates humanistic, biblical, theological, liturgical and ecclesial cultural areas – accompanies the concrete experience of the candidate's life without alienating her from the cultural context, according to an inner unification process. Formative areas are placed in the context of the principle of the unity of individual instructions that "converge in a profound under-

[16] Cf. Congregation for Institues of consecrated life and Societies of apostolic life, Directives on formation in religious institutes *Potissimum Institutioni,* Rome, (February 2, 1990), 79.

standing of the mystery of Christ"[17] and are entrusted to the discernment of the monastic authorities at every level, which, *servatis de jure servandis*, will always apply them with discretion and discernment, a virtue of the great western monastic tradition.

Aspirancy and postulancy

139. *Introduction to the Catholic faith.* It opens up the path of Christian discipleship for an introduction into the heart of the *kerygma*, namely "the ever fresh and attractive good news of the Gospel of Jesus Christ".[18] If deemed appropriate, a guided reading of the *Catechism of the Catholic Church* should be recommended, along with purifying and deepening the religious sensitivity of the candidates, guiding them to an understanding of the foundations of the faith as taught by the Magisterium.

140. *Fundamentals of anthropology.* Introducing candidates to a profound knowledge of the human person and of anthropology with

[17] FRANCIS, Ap. Const. *Veritatis gaudium*, (January 29, 2018), 70§1.

[18] FRANCIS, Ap. Ex. *Evangelii gaudium*, (November 24, 2013), 11; 34ss.

a *focus* on their own female identity placed in a reciprocal relation to the male one, according to the lifestyle of a female religious community. The accompaniment of experts, with targeted listening and personal evaluation, will be useful for a journey of human maturity.

141. *Introduction to the Holy Scriptures.* Introduction into the fundamental aspects of approaching the Word of God enshrined in the Scriptures: the literary genres, the exegetical foundations and the identification of references should provide a basic contextualisation of the texts.

142. *Introduction to lectio divina.* This path is not to be identified with the Introduction to Sacred Scripture, but rather with a process accompanying the entire monastic life as a prayerful and internal listening to the Word of God. Candidates will be introduced to reading the Bible, initiated into the literary genres starting with their own culture; guided to personal verbalization and to sharing the result of listening to the Scriptures. The scope of this study may also form part of the time devoted to the daily personal practice of *lectio* divina.

143. *Introduction to the liturgical year.* Due care must be given to the mystagogic path in accompanying the candidates to penetrate the liturgical year "in which the mysteries of the life of the Son of God are relived through His same inner attitudes"[19], to enjoy the wisdom of rituals, to understand the meaning of texts, to harmoniously embrace liturgical customs.

144. *Profiles of holiness.* The presentation of the spiritual profile of men and women who, in fidelity to the Gospel, have sought God in contemplative life to the point of holiness and martyrdom offers candidates the exemplariness of coherent witness lived in the radicality of following Christ. In particular, it involves an attitude of drawing close to "feminine styles of holiness, which are an essential means of reflecting God's holiness in this world".[20]

145. *Introduction to the spirituality of community service.* It involves helping candidates to develop

[19] Cf. CONGREGATION FOR INSTITUTES OF CONSECRATED LIFE AND SOCIETIES OF APOSTOLIC LIFE, *Starting Afresh from Christ: A renewed commitment to consecrated life in the Third Millennium*, (May 19, 2002),15

[20] FRANCIS, Ap. Ex. *Gaudete et exultate*, (March 19, 2018), 12.

a special sensitivity to work and service thereby enabling them to experience it as an inalienable human event, a source of sustenance, sharing and personal expression, "where many aspects of life enter into play: creativity, planning for the future, developing talents, living out values, relating to others, giving glory to God".[21]

146. *Introduction to humanistic culture.* Daily life shall be imbued with Christian humanism in harmony with the great monastic tradition, i.e. an active strategy for understanding the here and now. The challenges of contemporary society cannot be tackled outside the horizon of a humanistic culture whereby the complexity of knowledge and information is part of a broader vision. The introduction to classical culture, through the reading of its most relevant authors, and to pedagogical philosophy nurturing the identity of the *humanum* in a process of life directed towards the stature of Christ's humanity is therefore recommended.

147. *Knowledge of the particular Church.* Aspirants and postulants arriving at the monas-

[21] FRANCIS, *Laudato si'*, Encl. Letter on care for our Common Home, (2015), 127.

tery normally leave the country and Church of origin. They should thus be introduced to the particular Church (history, tradition, significant figures and realities of the Diocese) that is home to the monastery.

In the novitiate

148. *School of the Gospel.* The novitiate period is a privileged time to enter into intimate relationship with the mystery of our Lord Jesus. Continuous in-depth reflection on the words and gestures of Christ the Lord, as they are proclaimed in the Gospel, facilitates the conformity of the candidates' hearts to the feelings of Christ according to the Gospel.

149. *Introduction to the Psalter.* The daily practice of the Liturgy of the Hours, based on the Psalter, requires that during the novitiate this book be thoroughly examined as an integral model of Christian and monastic prayer. A personalized reading of the Psalms is essential and can be a fruitful apprenticeship to savour the mystery of prayer: it also educates to a prayerful attitude to the feelings of men and women of every age (joy, sadness, praise, reproach, hope, despair) in the path of deepening the personal intimacy with the Lord.

150. *Introduction to the study of the Rule and the Constitutions.* The novitiate leading up to the first religious profession is dedicated to the study of the *Rule* and the Constitutions, for they provide "a map for the whole journey of discipleship, in accordance with a specific charism confirmed by the Church. A greater regard for the Rule will not fail to offer consecrated persons a reliable criterion in their search for the appropriate forms of a witness which is capable of responding to the needs of the times without departing from an Institute's initial inspiration".[22]

151. *Introduction into the history and tradition of the monastery.* An in-depth study of the proper tradition, based on both spiritual and legislative texts, introduces the novices into a living tradition that grows and evolves within vital communities, with the contribution of new generations. In fact, "recounting our history is essential for preserving our identity, for strengthening our unity as a family and our common sense of belonging".

[22] JOHN PAUL II , Post-Synodal Ap. Ex. *Vita consecrata,* (March 25, 1996), 37

Learning the historical events of the Order, the Federation and, last but not least, the most significant biographies of the nuns of one's monastery means "following in the footsteps of past generations [...] to see how the charism has been lived over the years, the creativity it has sparked, the difficulties it encountered and the concrete ways those difficulties were surmounted. [...] To tell our story is to praise God and to thank him for all his gifts".[23]

152. *Formation to fraternal life.* The Church Magisterium, the theological-spiritual and anthropological reflection have incorporated the needs of community life into a perspective of fraternity, so as to foster a renewed sense of community life and of relationships experienced by consecrated women conscious of the fruitful tension between the ideal and the effort of community life. Fraternity is motivated by the desire to adhere to the practical nature of shared life *among* sisters, in the awareness of its specific feminine character recognized as a path of conversion towards fuller humanisation.

[23] FRANCIS, *Apostolic letter* to all consecrated people on the occasion of the Year of Consecrated Life, (November 21, 2014), I, 1.

153. *Musical and artistic education.* Candidates must be introduced not only to music and singing – in the context of a liturgical formation – but also to other artistic expressions or disciplines directed at expressing the creative potential of each one.

154. *Introduction to an ecological spirituality.* Care for our "common home"[24] is a precious legacy of the monastic tradition, premise of specific paths of formation in an ecological spirituality that "makes us more protective and respectful of the environment" and "it imbues our relationship to the world with a healthy sobriety".[25] This spirituality is also expressed in caring for the beauty of the common spaces which increase our sense of belonging, of rootedness, of "feeling at home" within the monastery and perceiving them as part of the "us" to be built together.[26]

During temporary profession

155. *Scriptures.* During the period of temporary profession, canonical books are to be

[24] FRANCIS, *Laudato si'*, Enc. Letter on care for our common home, (Rome, 2015), 13.

[25] *Ivi*, 126.

[26] *Ivi*, 151.

read in greater depth. It is recommended that they be supplemented with more specific biblical themes.

156. *Introduction to the Liturgy.* Introduction to the liturgical year must be continually deepened and expanded. It is necessary to begin with the meaning of myth and ritual in every culture, along with particular cultural and religious manifestations, leading up to Christian fulfilment. This approach allows for a full understanding of the mystery of the Liturgy and its creative adaptation at both personal and community levels.

157. *Introduction to reading the Church Fathers.* The temporary professed are guided in the study of Patristics. Beside detailed introductions, great space should be given to the direct reading of texts, thereby offering the nuns the taste for and the method of the *Lectio Patrum.*

158. *Introduction to Church history.* Introduction to the particular charism, begun during the novitiate, continues with a broad introduction to Church history. By doing so the nun, while feeling part of her own monastic reality, becomes increasingly involved in the complex and inspiring history of the Body of Christ which is the Church. Acquiring a historical sensitivity is necessary to courageously embrace the cultural challenges of the present and the future.

159. *Introduction to the texts of the Magisterium and the Second Vatican Council.* The knowledge of the texts and the context of the Second Vatican Council is a prerequisite for an adequate understanding of the Magisterium before and after Vatican II. Ecclesial communion requires an education to the *sentire cum Ecclesia*.

160. *Theology of consecrated and monastic life.* Monastic life is a particular and not superior expression of consecrated life as a form of fidelity to the one Baptism. This requires a careful study of the theology of consecrated and monastic life as a life of special consecration, personal and specific adherence to the common discipleship founded on baptism. Particular attention should be given to the contemplative charism in history and to the elements qualifying the choice for contemplative life.

161. *Introduction to the Schools of spirituality.* Temporary professed sisters should be introduced to the manifold richness of the work of the Spirit in the lives of the many men and women who have let themselves be won over by the Gospel. For this reason, it is of fundamental importance to present the other Schools of spirituality, to relativize and contextualize charismatic spirituality and be enriched by the different gifts and styles of fidelity to discipleship.

162. *Monastic interreligious dialogue.* In the Church, monastic life is a space open to dialogue, open to exchanges with other religions and cultures, while including anthropological and religious expressions of monastic life. This existential and experiential dialogue is necessary for monastic life and becomes a service practised on behalf of the Church. This commitment should envisage time for study and experience, through meetings and proximity.

163. *Fundamental principles of Canon law.* Canon law in its universal and particular expressions should not only be known in its direct applications to monastic life, it should also be presented as an incarnate and concrete expression of the burden of charity, the ultimate goal, *salus animarum*, of Canon law.

164. *Humanistic culture.* Further study of *auctores*, literature and pedagogical philosophy, of particular interest in contemporary culture, should be continued.

165. *Formation to media cultures.* As already broadly explained, communications and relationships today involve the use of the Internet. It is necessary to provide adequate formation in media culture and the use of its means of communication in order to prevent negative effects in the context of human and monastic formative identity. To this end, it is advisable to have targeted formation with the contribution of *ad hoc* experts.

166. *Personal or group areas.* During the period of temporary profession, other areas of interest can be identified and fostered, either individually or in small groups, ranging from horizons that open up to the learning of ancient languages used in scriptures and in patristic traditions; to far-reaching cultural and artistic interests such as poetry, music, iconic and manual arts. Over the centuries, monasteries have been centres of humanistic-Christian culture: in this regard, communities are required to discern community and personal needs, with openness of mind and heart.

Formation as desire and research

167. "Are you hastening toward your heavenly home? Then with Christ's help, keep this little rule that we have written for beginners".[27] The relationship with Jesus Christ must be nourished by the restlessness of the search. It makes us aware of the gratuitous gift of a vocation and it helps us to substantiate the reasons that motivated the initial choice and that remain in perseverance: "Letting Christ make us his own always means straining forward to what lies ahead, to the goal of Christ (cf. *Phil* 3:14)".[28]

This mystery lived in daily life calls for a personal response: "Faith is our response to a word which engages us personally, to a "Thou" who calls us by name"[29] and "as a response to a word which preceded it, it would always be an act of remembrance. Yet this remembrance is not fixed on past events but, as the memory of a promise, it becomes capable of opening up to the future, shedding light on the path to be tak-

[27] BENEDICT, *Rule*, 73, 8.

[28] FRANCIS, *Cammini creativi radicati nella Chiesa,* papa Francesco con i confratelli gesuiti nel giorno della memoria di sant'Ignazio di Loyola [*Homily on the occasion of the Feast of St. Ignatius, Church of the Gesù,* Rome, July 31, 2013], in: *L'Osservatore Romano,* Thursday Aug. 1, 2013, CLIII (175), p. 8.

[29] FRANCIS, Encyclical Letter *Lumen fidei*, (June 29, 2013), n. 8, in: *AAS* 105 (2013), 555-596.

en".[30] The search is continuous remembrance of being called here and now to a unified monastic personality, harmoniously open to all dimensions of life. Each sister in responsible discernment is made a wise scribe who, being *trained for the kingdom of heaven, is like the master of a household who brings out of his treasure what is new and what is old* (*Matt.* 13:52). An ever-thriving path, in the way of the bride of the Canticles: *Have you seen him whom my soul loves?* (*Ct* 3:3). In our quest, Love leads us to the encounter.

Mary, *summa contemplatrix*

168. Our thoughts turn to Mary, a woman rooted in silence, a *virgin made Church*, a temple in which the Word and the voice of the Spirit reverberate like a light aura: "It was conceded that, in a singular way, by her and through her the mysteries of human salvation would be fulfilled, so she was allowed to contemplate them in an eminent and deeper way".[31] From the invitation to *Rejoice*, *All Beautiful*, to the custody of

[30] *Ivi*, n. 9.

[31] S. De Fiores, *In Praise of Contemplation*, in S. M. Pasini (Ed.), *Mary, model of contemplation of the mystery of Christ*, Ed. Monfortane, Rome 2000, 21-22.

the events that reveal the mystery in our daily life; from the *peregrinatio* along the Via Dolorosa to the *statio iuxta crucem*; from the deep silence of the Sabbath to the dawn of the Risen One, Mary is made *summa contemplatrix, capax Dei.*

And so may it be for every contemplative woman: in the silence of the cloister, inhabited by mystery, may she beget life.

On June 9, 2019, the Holy Father approved the present document of the Congregation for Institutes of Consecrated Life and Societies of Apostolic Life and authorized its publication.

Vatican City, August 15th 2019
Solemnity of the Assumption of the Blessed Virgin Mary

João Braz Card. de Aviz
Prefect

✠ José Rodríguez Carballo, O.F.M.
Archbishop Secretary

Appendix

Concrete aspects of human, Christian and charismatic growth

The aspects of human and Christian growth develop as one in practical life, even if theoretically different.

Among the most important aspects of human and Christian growth, formation places particular attention on the following:

1. Aspects of human growth

a. Regarding the person

- ✓ knowledge, self-acceptance and sense of identity;
- ✓ sense of personal freedom, initiative and responsibility for personal life;
- ✓ ability to discern, decide and be committed;
- ✓ engagement in physical, psychological, moral, spiritual and social growth, morally and spiritually;
- ✓ emotional and affective balance;
- ✓ ability to transcend and overcome egocentricity;

- ✓ awareness and acceptance of the gift of one's own sexuality and desire to embrace chastity;
- ✓ availability for manual work;
- ✓ openness and receptivity to new values, attitudes, perspectives and experiences;
- ✓ ability to accept, live, dialogue and work with others, even from different cultures;
- ✓ sense of justice and peace;
- ✓ ability to show solidarity towards the poor;
- ✓ honesty and loyalty;
- ✓ joy and happiness.

b. *Regarding the community*

- ✓ ability to develop positive interpersonal relationships with other sisters;
- ✓ ability to communicate and deal with conflicts in a positive way;
- ✓ spirit of cooperation;
- ✓ openness and flexibility.

c. *Regarding the world*

- ✓ ability to read the "signs of the times";
- ✓ solidarity with the poor and marginalised.

2. Aspects of Christian growth

a. Regarding God

- ✓ sense of gratitude;
- ✓ desire for continuous conversion;
- ✓ life of faith, translated into word and action, and of hope;
- ✓ growth in unconditional love;
- ✓ searching for God's will in all things;
- ✓ willingness to seek and do God's will;
- ✓ willingness to pray and become a person centred in God;
- ✓ personal relationship with Jesus Christ, nourished by the regular celebration of the Sacraments and by reflection on His Word, and a serious commitment to follow Him;
- ✓ knowledge of the Catholic faith and love for the Church;
- ✓ awareness of God's presence and His redeeming action in personal life, in the Church and in the world;
- ✓ willingness to be evangelized and to evangelize through the witness of life and word as contemplatives;
- ✓ prophetic, missionary and ecumenical spirit.

b. Regarding the Church-world relationship

- ✓ sense of God's presence in the world;
- ✓ knowledge of the Catholic faith;
- ✓ love for the Catholic Church;
- ✓ missionary and ecumenical spirit;
- ✓ search for justice and peace.

3. Aspects of growth according to the proper charism

a. Regarding God

- ✓ following of Christ, humble and poor;
- ✓ radical evangelical life;
- ✓ life of penitence;
- ✓ spirit of prayer and devotion.

b. Regarding the community/fraternity

- ✓ love for one's proper community;
- ✓ love and understanding for each sister;
- ✓ fraternal service, especially to elderly and sick sisters;
- ✓ mutual loving obedience;
- ✓ overcoming selfishness, self-will and the forces that hinder the development of the community/fraternity;
- ✓ willingness to work manually;
- ✓ active participation in community and fraternal life.

c. *Regarding the Church-world relationship*

- ✓ love for the Church;
- ✓ charitable obedience to the Shepherds;
- ✓ evangelization and mission;
- ✓ prophetic spirit;
- ✓ preferential option for the poor;
- ✓ commitment to reconciliation and forgiveness;
- ✓ respect for nature and the environment.

INDEX

www.ingramcontent.com/pod-product-compliance
Ingram Content Group UK Ltd.
Pitfield, Milton Keynes, MK11 3LW, UK
UKHW041952190726
13854UKWH00005B/1920

9 788826 604770